Effective Personal Communication Skills for Public Relations

Dedicated to Alan Rawel – sorry you didn't get to see my memes come true; to Jim Britton, who helped me with his candour and kindness; and to Amanda Marsh – you're never forgotten.

PR IN PRACTICE SERIES

Effective Personal Communication Skills for Public Relations

Andy Green

CHARTERED INSTITUTE OF PUBLIC RELATIONS

KOGAN PAGE

London and Philadelphia

Publisher's note

Every possible effort has been made to ensure that the information contained in this book is accurate at the time of going to press, and the publishers and author cannot accept responsibility for any errors or omissions, however caused. No responsibility for loss or damage occasioned to any person acting, or refraining from action, as a result of the material in this publication can be accepted by the editor, the publisher or the author.

First published in Great Britain and the United States in 2006 by Kogan Page Limited

120 Pentonville Road
London N1 9JN
United Kingdom
www.kogan-page.co.uk

525 South 4th Street, #241
Philadelphia PA 19147
USA

© Andy Green, 2006

ISBN 0 7494 4407 X

British Library Cataloguing-in-Publication Data

A CIP record for this book is available from the British Library.

Library of Congress Cataloging-in-Publication Data

Green, Andy, 1958–
    Effective personal communication skills for public relations / Andy Green.
        p. cm.
    Includes index.
    ISBN 0-7494-4407-X
    1. Public relations. 2. Communication. 3. Influence (Psychology) I. Title.
HD59.G684 2006
659.201'4—dc22
                2006008147

Typeset by JS Typesetting Ltd, Porthcawl, Mid Glamorgan
Printed and bound in the United States by Thomson-Shore, Inc

Contents

PR in Practice Series

Published in association with the Chartered Institute of Public Relations
Series Editor: Anne Gregory

Kogan Page has joined forces with the Chartered Institute of Public Relations to publish this unique series which is designed specifically to meet the needs of the increasing numbers of people seeking to enter the public relations profession and the large band of existing PR professionals. Taking a practical, action-oriented approach, the books in the series concentrate on the day-to-day issues of public relations practice and management rather than academic history. They provide ideal primers for all those on CIPR, CAM and CIM courses or those taking NVQs in PR. For PR practitioners, they provide useful refreshers and ensure that their knowledge and skills are kept up to date.

Professor Anne Gregory is one of the UK's leading public relations academics. She is Director of the Centre for Public Relations Studies at Leeds Metropolitan University. Before becoming an academic, Anne spent 12 years in public relations practice and has experience at a senior level both in-house and in consultancy. She remains involved in consultancy work and is a non-executive director of South West Yorkshire Mental Health NHS Trust with special responsibility for communication issues. Anne initiated the *PR in Practice* series and is the Consultant Editor. She edited the book of the same name and wrote and *Planning and Managing a Public Relations Campaign*, also in this series. She was President of the CIPR in 2004.

Other titles in the series:

Forthcoming titles:

The above titles are available from all good bookshops and from the CIPR website www.cipr.co.uk/books To obtain further information, please contact the publishers at the address below:

Kogan Page Ltd
120 Pentonville Road
London N1 9JN
Tel: 020 7278 0433 Fax: 020 7837 6348
www.kogan-page.co.uk

Foreword

Public relations is just that: it's about forming relationships with a variety of publics such as customers, the local community, stakeholders, the media or even with key individuals.

Critical to success is not only having a good plan with realistic objectives and a tactical programme to support it, but a keen sense of the human dimension. To develop meaningful and long-lasting relationships requires a clear understanding of people; what makes them tick, what motivates them and what makes them respond. They might not always respond how you want them to, but that is in the nature of relationships. Getting a response means that at least you have communicated.

This book focuses on what might be called the softer science and art of public relations. As such it goes alongside the other books in the series which provide fuller explanations on the detailed practicalities of planning and implementing the various functional areas of public relations practice.

The book talks about individual practitioners themselves. What their personal beliefs and values are and how they think. It then examines how they interact with others; what their interpersonal skills are, how they create meaningful communication and how they use networks, of all kinds, effectively.

It also looks at the context in which communicators operate and how that shapes the effectiveness of what they do. I guess only Andy Green could finish with a story combining a computer nerd and Jesus, but I won't give the ending away!

In an age where sophisticated planning, payment by results and 'contribution to the bottom line' are all important, it's sometimes easy to forget that our business is all about making connections with people. People are complex, unpredictable and infinitely demanding and uniquely rewarding. So is our work. By developing the skills proposed in this book, not only will we be judged by the quality and professionalism of our work, but we will find that we will become those well-rounded and effective communicators that are talked about with warmth as well as admiration.

Anne Gregory

Acknowledgements

Many thanks to the beta readers who made this a better book:

Anne Akers, North Kirklees Primary Care Trust
Andrew Dunne, Dunne Good consultancy
Marc Evans, Civitas Cymru
Richard Jones, faragher//jones publishing
Nathan Lane, Golley Slater
David Marsh, *Yorkshire Evening Post*
Adrian Mahoney, PR Store
Daniel Phillips, GREEN communications
Alan Preece, University of East Anglia
Geoff Roberts, Hidden Resources
David Taylor, creativity@work
John Timperley, Winning business
Heather Yaxley, Applause Consultancy

Thanks too of course to series editor Anne Gregory and Gro Elin Hansen of the Chartered Institute of Public Relations for their unstinting patience and support.

Sprint summary

Quickly find out what is in this book by reading either the 'sprint' summary below or the 'jog' version after Chapter 11.

Chapter 1   Your inner brand – who you are

How you think shapes all your communications. You are a living brand. This is at the heart of your success as a PR communicator and your communications campaigns.

Chapter 2   Your communications quotient – your thinking resources

Your type of thinking is marked by the qualities and depth of your different quotients in intelligence, emotional, adversity and vision coupled with your ability to secure the optimum balance between them for the different situations you face as a communicator.

Chapter 3   You and your interpersonal skills

You communicate with every part of your body and your actions.

Chapter 4   Creating messages, memes and 'spinning'

You need to revolutionize your communications thinking beyond messages with just a sender and a recipient; messages possess an inherent dynamic enabling them to live on beyond. This dynamic is called a *meme*. Everyone 'spins' in their communications using three different tactics.

Chapter 5   The message is the medium – making your communications brand-friendly

The way you structure and shape your message will make it memorable and enable it to live on, and on.

Chapter 6   Triggering your message to achieve change

You can use a number of techniques to enable your messages to create change.

Chapter 7   Adapting your messages to your networks – word-of-mouth and word-of-click, your viral friends

You can manage word of mouth. Pass it on.

New online technology can hyper spread your word of mouth. Please forward.

You need to adapt your communications to your different networks.

Chapter 8   Your networks

It's not what you know but who you know – the few right people on your side can create a tidal wave of communications. Your connections in most cases will provide an answer to your problems. You are probably no more than four contacts away from anyone on this planet.

Chapter 9   Managing your networking

You can manage your networking and improve your skills to achieve greater results from this unrecognized marketing discipline.

Chapter 10   The power of context – managing the environment for your communications

No matter how good your communications its value will be determined by its context. But you can manage this.

Chapter 11   Bringing it all together

Two case studies examine how one person can create tidal waves of communications.

There is a more detailed summary at the end of the book called 'The quick read – the jog'.

Introduction

From one note a million vibrations can be created.

John Coltrane

At the heart of public relations practice is the individual. A tidal wave of communications can stem from just one person; one person sneezes and the world can catch a cold.

Is it possible to identify the key skills used by outstanding public relations communicators? Can their intrinsic qualities be harnessed by others, whether you are new to the profession or an experienced professional seeking to extend your capabilities? *Effective Communication Skills for Public Relations* empowers readers with personal strategies for effective communications. It analyses how you can transform your communications by managing the way you think, act, create messages and network.

The book provides practical guidance on understanding the different facets to making communications happen. It covers the processes under-pinning negotiating skills, conflict resolution, defusing emotion, effective client management and many other so-called 'soft skills' of communications practice.

It is also a valuable guide to understanding new trends and challenges facing communicators in an 'information obese' era, including how intra-personal and interpersonal communications operate and how you are a 'living brand'; how you can manage word of mouth – and now word of click – communications; how beliefs and values systems – which are expressed through your actions and behaviours – can be defined and shaped; how you operate within a series of networks containing different 'opinion formers'; how ideas and information are transmitted rather like viruses. Readers will gain an understanding of the processes and tools for managing individual mass communications, or 'sneeze communications', in their work.

The book lays claim to recognizing activities such as networking and word of mouth communications as being part of public relations practice. It is a book to make you reflect on how you operate as a public relations practitioner, and to change your thinking and doing.

1

Your inner brand – who you are

The most powerful voice you have, no one else can hear. It is a voice shaping your destiny, ability to cope with triumph or disaster, and how you engage with and inspire others in any quest you face. This voice ultimately determines your success as a communicator and the success of your communications. It is the voice within your head.

The starting point for being an outstanding public relations communicator is recognizing that you deliver communications not just through your words, signs or gestures. Nor do you deliver just through your body language. You communicate through the way you think.

You probably know of people who can easily comment on other people's problems but are blind to their own shortcomings. The ability to understand yourself, your own emotions, and know how your mind works is known as your intrapersonal skill. Having a self-awareness and understanding of yourself makes it possible subsequently to develop fully your interpersonal skills. Your intrapersonal skill is essentially how you can manage your own thinking – the ability to understand how your thinking works and ultimately master the voice in your head.

Everyone has an inner voice that creates an internal dialogue, a self-talk, which shapes and progresses their thinking and communication. (Your self-talk is not a sign of delusional behaviour!) This self-talk lies at the heart of your subsequent communications. If you are unclear in your mind about how you feel and understand about an issue, the probability is that your subsequent communications will reflect this uncertainty, or fail to convince.

The image of Sir Bob Geldof when he launched Band Aid in 1984 is a good of example of someone with a clear sense of passion and belief, who initially had limited resources – at the outset his campaign was just him and his intense reaction to watching BBC news coverage of famine scenes in Ethiopia. Yet he succeeded in creating a major brand and raising valuable funds for famine relief. His clear sense of purpose fuelled his passion to overcome the odds. A committed community activist can likewise often outwit and perform a well-oiled and well-funded formal public relations programme; witness the success of groups like Greenpeace against major oil companies.

The potential of the focused few was recognized by sociologist Margaret Mead: 'Never doubt that a small group of thoughtful committed citizens can change the world. Indeed, it is the only thing that ever has' (Howard, 1984). The starting point for your journey in understanding and becoming an outstanding public relations communicator is to examine what shapes your thinking and how it is manifested in your communications.

PHYSIOLOGY PART ONE

Before you read any further, examine the way you are sitting or standing. Stretch your body and create a feeling of being wide awake. Now you have the personal energy to proceed with the right level of concentration.

'INFORMATION': THE FIRST STEP IN UNDERSTANDING YOUR INTRAPERSONAL SKILLS

In order to manage your intrapersonal skills you need to understand how your brain interacts with the world around you. Imagine your brain is like a sponge, absorbing 'information' from its surrounding environment. According to psychologist George A. Miller (1956), your conscious brain can handle around 500 bits of information every minute. This might seem pretty impressive, yet it pales into insignificance compared with your ability to accommodate fresh deliveries of over 2 million bits of information a minute at an unconscious level.

In public relations practice 'information' tends to be defined solely as hard facts, like 'What is the size of your organization?' or 'What products do you sell?' Information is in reality a much broader concept, consisting of data that engages and interacts with any of our senses – sight, sound, smell, taste and touch – as well as our intellectual and emotional capacities. This data could be sensing someone else's mood or feeling. It could be gaining an impression of whether to trust a person. As my wife commented on someone who had behaved less than ethically, 'I knew we shouldn't have trusted her after she served tinned carrots for dinner!'

Your data gathering at an unconscious level is more effective than your conscious mind in absorbing larger volumes of information and also more profound, higher-grade data. Someone, or an organization, might say to you, 'Trust us', but intuitively your instincts might register a feeling of, 'There's something about that person or organization I don't trust.' This message could exist within your mind as an explicit statement saying, 'Don't trust this person or organization!' The message can also exist as an underlying, non-articulated mood, a general sense of something you cannot quite be specific about, but it is a sign for you to potentially recognize, and base your subsequent actions on.

Nonverbal communications can obtain data about wider emotional/ relational matters rather than material facts, offering more truthful insights into what lies behind the verbal message. They are like a 'window on the soul'. Some of your biggest decisions, such as falling in love, are based on intuition. Although your intuitive feelings might not be consciously, coherently or explicitly stated, learn to recognize the signals your body creates in registering these non-articulated feelings. A key characteristic of outstanding public relations practitioners is they always, always trust their instincts.

When 'listening' to your intuition, take care to distinguish intuitive signals based purely on fear. Also check whether the intuitive feelings you have are relevant to the question you face. A personal experience of mine illustrates this point. I once made a bad decision on a job appointment based on the feeling that the person I was thinking of employing was a 'nice guy'. My intuition was not at fault: the chap was indeed a nice guy, and still is. He was however, less than good for the job. I should have used a more tightly defined question of 'Can this person cope with the specific demands of the job?' to act as a counterbalance against any intuitive feelings.

A simple tool for helping to provoke and articulate intuitive feelings is to first frame the problem you face as a 'Yes' or 'No' option. Then toss a coin to make a decision – heads you do it, tails you don't. If the coin flips to heads it might prompt the voice in your head to think, 'Maybe I should toss it one more time.' This is your intuition advising you either that this is the wrong decision, or that it is the wrong time to make a decision.

Task: putting it into practice

Think back to when you have had a 'gut feeling' about something: did you listen and respond to this feeling? How perceptive was this information? Think about any bad decision you have made. Did you in fact have warnings that you failed to listen to or interpret?

MENTAL MAPS: YOUR PERCEPTION OF 'REALITY'

Having soaked up information from your surrounding environment, your mind creates your own mental map of what you perceive as 'reality'. This mental map is like a theatre stage offering the backdrop, the setting and context within which you act your role in the world. It provides you with your script to guide your actions and communications.

How you perceive this stage setting, your role within it, and your script is personal and unique to you. That is why no two outstanding public relations communicators are the same. Your mental map is different from the mental map of anyone else you are trying to communicate with. Your maps are useful, but are not necessarily right in their interpretation of the world around you. The London Underground map of the tube system, for example, bears a limited relationship to the geography of London. It is however, a very useful tool to enable you to get around its world.

Your unique mental map of the world is a wonderful creation but does have its flaws. Your unique mental maps will inevitably be incomplete:

- Whatever you do, or say, will be misunderstood in some way.
- You will misunderstand whatever you see, sense, feel or hear in some way.

The fundamental starting point for the effective communicator is recognizing that all communications at an individual level and in any public relations campaign are inherently flawed because you operate within your own unique mental map of the world. As a public relations communicator your communications must work to minimize misunderstanding, and enhance potential understanding.

Michael Bland, a leading UK expert on communications, reflects on the failure to understand other people's mental maps:

> In my experience the most startling flops in public relations stem from a failure to recognize that other people will inevitably see the world different to you; from major companies failing to understand the mentality of activists

opposing them, or managers in the middle of a crisis not taking into account what people really want to hear rather than what just suits them. These all originate from an insularity of thinking, and operating within just one world view.

Task: putting it into practice

What are the key elements creating, shaping and moulding your mental map, or your organization's? When you are negotiating, managing others, or seeking to resolve a conflict, do you recognize that other people's mental maps are different to yours? How are they different?

BELIEFS AND VALUES

To develop your intrapersonal skills you need to understand what shapes our individual mental maps. The mental maps we create in our minds have a shape and form. Imagine your mental map of the world is like a big tent. Beliefs and values act as your tent poles.

Beliefs

Beliefs are things you hold to be true, even if sometimes faced with evidence to the contrary. You may feel the sports team you support is the greatest in the world, although their actual real-world performance and results might not substantiate this case!

Beliefs are generalizations you make about yourself, other people and the world around you, and they provide a feeling of certainty, a touchstone, about what something means to you. Beliefs determine how you think and feel, what you will do or not do, how you feel about anything in your life. They are the principles by which you act. As soon as you have a belief it begins to control what you see and what you feel.

The backbone of the way outstanding public relations practitioners act is their core beliefs. Beliefs such as 'I love my family' or a spiritual belief in a higher being play a prime role in your life. These beliefs govern the way you choose to live and act, and are difficult to change. They can range from attitudes to life – 'Things will get better/worse' – and your skills – 'I'm good/no good' – to less significant beliefs pervading your life – 'I believe butter is better/worse than margarine.'

The adage 'Whether you believe you can or you can't do, you're right' is indicative of how beliefs act as self-fulfilling prophecies. This factor of making themselves come true gives beliefs their power. Beliefs can act as useful, empowering permissions that enable you to fulfil your potential. Equally, other beliefs can act as unnecessary self-limiting brakes. The question to ask of any belief is, 'Is it useful and does it serve me?'

Powerful beliefs for communicators include:

- There is no failure, only feedback. If you are faced with a result or outcome different from what was initially intended, switching the label of 'failure' to the term 'feedback' overcomes a sense of negativity. It creates a potentially valuable learning experience from which you can modify any future actions. Next time a campaign does not achieve the results you hoped for, assess what you could have done differently: what lessons are there to be learnt, and what you will do differently next time.
- The meaning of communication is the response you get. If you blame the audience for not 'getting' your message, or 'misunderstanding' a part of your mental map, you are effectively taking away your ability to respond flexibly, to change your communications to ensure your message is understood. In a failure in negotiations, or managing staff or clients, shift your analysis away from any suggestion that they are the 'problem'. Instead, examine what you should have done differently to get your message understood by the target audience.
- The intention of other people's behaviour is positive. Every action they take is the best choice available to them at the time, given their mental map. It might be incomprehensible to you, but it is real to them. By understanding how a person's mental map works you can find the positive intention behind any 'difficult' behaviour. With this knowledge of the other person's model you can understand where he or she is coming from, so you have the choice to manage your response accordingly.

Although beliefs are powerful, they can be changed. Do you believe in Father Christmas? Probably not as an adult, but you did when you were a child. Think back to your childhood when your belief about Father Christmas was absolute. The character of Santa Claus is what is known as an intentional object – a made-up creature of beliefs which can play a more direct role in guiding people's behaviours than real objects. (Chapters 5 and 6 will examine how to shape messages to change beliefs.)

As a communicator you need to identify the extent of your beliefs, or your organization's, and those of your target audience. When you communicate by doing this 'belief check' you can have a profound insight into the mental maps of both yourself and your target audiences.

One of the most important beliefs when you are doing a presentation is that you as an individual communicator have the right to be addressing the audience. The most successful communicators possess this belief, and it manifests itself in their body language. (See Chapter 3.)

When the UK government in 2004 held a referendum for creating a new tier of regional government in the north of England it provided an example of how beliefs can influence the success or failure of a campaign. I was involved in the 'Yes' campaign for the Yorkshire region. Although a referendum was eventually held only in the North-East region (which met with a resounding 'No' vote), the failure of the 'Yes' campaigns was ultimately down to beliefs: committed 'Yes' supporters were basing their support on the principle of devolved regional government rather than the detail of the specific proposal actually offered to the electorate. Their lack of belief in the product they were selling made itself manifest in their subsequent campaign, failing to generate an evangelical zeal for their message.

An interesting insight into the low self-belief of the public relations profession is provided by David Yelland, the former editor of the *Sun*, the UK's largest-selling daily newspaper, and now senior vice chairman of Weber Shandwick. He comments, 'The PR industry has a low self-confidence. We pitch far too low, whether it is the fees we charge as consultants or about the impact our product contributes to business success.'

Task: putting it into practice

How many campaigns have you been involved with where the presence or lack of belief ultimately had an impact on the success or otherwise of the communications?

Values

If beliefs are the hard and fast reference points – the upright poles for keeping our metaphorical tent up – values are the horizontal poles and tent pegs holding the tent together, giving it the space to engage flexibly with the wider world. A value is best defined as something you will do even if it hurts. Values are the things that are important to you in your life. By valuing something you place importance on it. In the same way that everyone has individual beliefs, each of us has different values. As a communicator you are likely to put a high value on connecting with people, building understanding, and securing dialogue and engagement in the minds of others.

Your core values permeate most of what you do, and provide the key to understanding what you do and why you do it. Your values filter any information you gather. If for example you do not value diversity, this will influence your behaviours: you will not be gathering information from diverse sources because your values will shape your world-view and you perceive these as irrelevant.

Each of us has different values. You also have a hierarchy of values, what can be called the rule number one syndrome. If you have a number of tasks, which of these tasks automatically takes precedence over the others? The things you do first tend to relate to the higher-order values.

The challenge in identifying your values is that far too often people confuse empty platitudes with values: take for example the corporate mantra 'We put our customers first.' Remember a value is what you do even when it hurts. If you really do put customers first, are you prepared to take a reduced income or even a financial loss on a job to ensure customer satisfaction? If this is not what happens in reality, then it is not a value, or it is one that is lower in your values hierarchy than the value of achieving financial goals.

Values tend to be hard to pin down. How can you identify an underlying value to your actions and communications? When you are faced with an ill-defined problem, a technique to overcome this fuzziness is to examine what is the opposite of something you value. What are the things you do not care about? It can be easier to spot the things where your actions are non-existent or are poor in performance. These areas of indifference make up your 'complacency zone', marking out the areas where you fail to, or are disinclined to act. Your complacency zone is a good way of defining your values; defining what you are not helps define what you are.

Money, or some form of materialism, is often wrongly cited as a prime value for most people. Other than those at the very bottom of the economic spectrum, research shows people generally do not work more for monetary rewards, except when the task is very easy and not very interesting. Intrinsic motivation is driven by a task having some form of relevant meaning to you: you might want to demonstrate your professional capabilities, prove yourself to someone, or give the task some wider reference and relate it to something you feel is important in your life – a value.

When communicating you need to check the compatibility of the values contained within the communication with the recipient's existing values. If an idea seems well founded to most people exposed to it and does not compromise their values, they are more likely to adopt and retain that new communication. You accept inner responsibility for behaviour when you think you have chosen to perform it in the absence of strong outside pressure.

A good example of using values in public relations campaigns is the linking of a campaign with a charity or good cause, such as affinity marketing. By aligning yourself with what the charity stands for – its values – you are aiming to create a bridge with your audience's values. (Chapter 5 has more on how to shape values in your messages.)

Warburtons, the family bakers and one of the UK's top grocery brands, is a good example of a company which recognizes the importance of managing values in its communications.

Andrea Law, brand communications manager at Warburtons, describes one of the tactics they use:

> We recognize that to be a successful brand we need to be true to our values. These must be demonstrated by all employees – not just in marketing communications. Therefore, we have published our own 'little book of values' to ensure we all understand how important the values of this family business are to achieving our many goals. In turn, this naturally translates itself into our brand communication.

ATTITUDE STATE

In the analogy of a tent representing your personal mental map, attitudes are the equivalent of the tent's canvas, providing the broad swathe of interaction between you and the outside environment. Attitudes are an expression of your underlying values and beliefs. They reflect how you feel about something, what you like or dislike, and provide a guide to expressing your behaviour in relation to a task. Information alone does not change attitudes. The reality, and shortcoming, of much public relations communications is that it focuses only on the information level. The communicator needs to engage with underlying beliefs and values in some way to effect a change in attitudes.

Whenever you communicate, your actions and the way you handle how you receive feedback will be framed by your attitude state. There are four broad attitude states which spur on, or spurn, any new information you receive (Figure 1.1). I have defined these attitude or perception states as first, the confidence you perceive in your abilities or the success you are perceived to be experiencing, and second, the flexibility with which you respond to new information.

A *hubris* mental state is marked by a perception of enjoying success, prompting a sense of arrogance and conviction in one's abilities, and ultimately omnipotence. As a result it is coupled with inflexibility, a blindness to looking around for new opportunities or ideas, and a deafness to listening to challenging advice. It is a mental state characterized as success before the fall.

Corporate hubris is probably one of the key reasons that public relations practitioners have been held back in gaining access and influence in higher boardroom positions. Effective public relations counsel identifying potential threats, negative undercurrents and damage to corporate reputation (and ultimately corporate success) is often overlooked as being a nebulous, non-credible risk when seen from a hubris mental state.

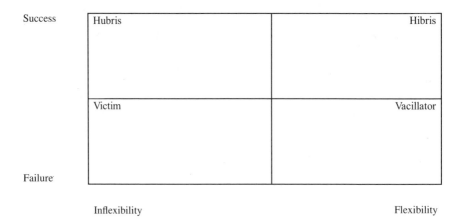

Figure 1.1 *Attitude states*

For an example of corporate example of hubris, take the UK retailer Marks & Spencer. During the 1990s the company was held up as a benchmark, with many a management conference told, 'We want to be the Marks & Spencer of our sector.' The company was subsequently guilty of failing to respond to new developments in the marketplace, partly blinded by its earlier success.

A *victim* mental state is characterized by a permanent and pervasive pessimism: whatever is done, there will be a problem. Once during a creativity session with a regional police force I was asked to devise a technique for coming up with ideas to address potential negative media coverage for a forthcoming quarterly crime statistics report. 'We know we will get criticized and blamed when they are published,' a delegate ruefully remarked. I asked, 'Is it your police officers who are committing all these crimes? If not, why are you making yourself 100 per cent accountable for something you are not 100 per cent in charge of?'

Victims are on a downward self-reinforcing spiral of negative thinking. Whatever they do, they will fail. From my personal experience, many practitioners working in parts of the public sector face the constraint of a widespread 'victim' culture, which supports a negative attitude to change.

A *hibris* mental state is like hubris, employing a positive arrogance on its ability to achieve success. Yet in a hibris state the arrogance is focused on the ability to be successful but tempered with humility. Those with hibris don't know everything, and there is a flexibility of thought and respect that there is always something to learn from even from the unlikeliest of sources.

The hibris state recognizes that your mental models are best guesses, and so you should be on the lookout for different ones. When confronted with problems, look at the assumptions behind the situation (see Chapter 4 on paradigms). Look for relationships, and how events fit together, and consider what are the causes and effects in the situation you are examining. Because of its diversity and breadth of interests a hibris state is more comfortable with ambiguity and maintains a curiosity with the outside world. It pays particular attention to experiences which contradict your mental models, and seeks to obtain constructive feedback to learn from any experience.

Douglas Smith of Westminster Advisers has had extensive experience of working with communicators in his lobbying career:

> The most successful operators are those who are not only flexible but also quick in their thinking. One of my heroes from the history books is F E Smith [Lord Birkenhead], who has entered more dictionaries of political quotations than most. One of his best known is his response to a challenge made for regularly using the rest room of a famous London Club, of which he was not a member. Asked by an awed head porter, 'Are you a member of this club, sir?' he replied, 'Good God, is it a club as well?'

A *vacillator* mental state recognizes something needs to be done but lacks a focus on where to obtain new inspiration, and a lack of conviction in applying new learning and delivering results. Unless vacillators secure a hibris state there is a danger they will eventually fall into a victim state.

Using this attitude state model you can identify if there is a potential willingness for you or your target audience to accept new information. No matter how coherent or well articulated your case, your communications will fail if there is a resilient hubris or victim culture among your target audience. You can only change attitudes by connecting with your target's beliefs and values.

Some simple check questions to use for checking attitude states include 'Is your target audience willing to embrace new ideas or consider new directions?' and 'How permanent and pervasive are any negative views held by your audience?'

Task: putting it into practice

Think about any recent communications you were involved with at an individual or campaign level. What were the attitude states of you and your target audience? In what ways were they different, and how did they affect the success or failure of the communications? Did you identify any different beliefs, values or attitudes from your own? Did you think about how your own beliefs, values and attitudes affected your communications?

PHYSIOLOGY PART TWO

What has happened to your physiology in the 10 minutes or so since you were last asked this question earlier in the chapter? Your body posture will shape the way you think. If you are slumped, with your head hanging down, you are less likely to be as positive and self-assured as someone adopting a more alert stance. Managing your physiology will help you manage the way you think.

THE CORNERSTONE OF YOUR COMMUNICATIONS: YOUR THINKING

Your skill as a public relations communicator will depend on what is important to you about communications, and why you do this job. Your skill as a communicator comes from what you do, your behaviour, underpinned by your core beliefs and values. These core beliefs and values underlie your identity: who you perceive yourself to be, and what your mission in life is. Is communication just something you happen to do, or do you think of yourself as a communicator?

Beliefs, values and your sense of identity help determine your own personal brand. Your personal brand is the launch pad from which you launch your communications to the outer world. (Chapter 5 covers the key elements that shape your brand, and also how you can manage these elements to improve the effectiveness of your communications.)

PR FUTURES DEBATE

Should public relations professionals be responsible for managing an organization's beliefs and values?

Should beliefs and values audits be common practice, feature in public relations practice, and be linked to your corporate social responsibility programmes?

PERSONAL CHECKLIST

- Think about how good your intrapersonal skills are. How well do you know yourself?
- What is your personal brand – as defined by your beliefs and values – in your organization or with your clients?

Task: putting it into practice

At what level (see Table 1.1) do you personally manage your beliefs and values? You can also apply this checklist to yourself and your organization.

Table 1.1 *Levels for managing your beliefs and values*

Level	What it means
Unconscious incompetent	Not aware of beliefs and values as issues in your communication
Conscious incompetence	Know that you are not aware of beliefs and values but lack the skills to address and manage this dimension
Conscious competence	Know about the significance of beliefs and values and have to consciously work at managing them
Unconscious competence	Implicitly live and breathe beliefs values in all actions. You do it without thinking about it.
Conscious super-competence	Recognize that beliefs and values are integral to success and consciously address and invest in your superlative performance in this area

---

- What is your attitude state when communicating?
- What are your beliefs/values?

PRELUDE TO CHAPTER 2

Your style of thinking is marked by the qualities and depth of your different quotients in intelligence, emotional, adversity and vision coupled with your ability to secure the optimum balance between them. Your thinking resources create your own communications quotient. Successful communicators call upon different qualities at different times to overcome obstacles to their communications.

2

Your communications quotient – your thinking resources

Your style of thinking and the unique way you communicate are determined by the qualities and depth of your different quotients in intelligence, emotional, adversity and vision, coupled with your ability to secure the optimum balance between them. Different situations will require different types of thinking.

The concept of intelligence quotient is well known as one measure of someone's ability. It is however only one yardstick of identifying your capability. You also have quotients in your emotional, vision and adversity skills which, when working together with your intelligence, enable you to create ideas to communicate.

Your 'brand' of thinking, the distinctive way you think as an individual, is shaped by how you use these different quotients. Every communication challenge is different, with each situation demanding different approaches. In some cases you will need to emphasize facts and details; other times you need to engage emotionally with your audience, or inspire, or be prepared to fight it out.

Your *communications quotient* (CQ) is your ability to use your various quotients to devise and deliver communications for the task at hand. The outstanding public relations communicator is marked by being flexible and being able to secure the optimum balance between these different resources to meet the needs of a specific time or situation.

Different communicators will be suited to different situations, because of their varying strengths in their resource quotients. A dynamic, powerful orator may be ideal for leading a group, but in another context someone who is low-key, trusting and can empathize may be more appropriate.

THE FOUR QS

The four quotients can be visualized as the four points of a diamond, as in Figure 2.1. How do these different quotients work, and how can communicators use them in their communications?

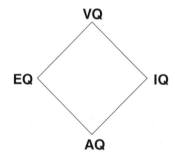

Figure 2.1 *The four quotients*

INTELLIGENCE QUOTIENT (IQ)

Your ability to analyse, rationalize and retain knowledge is often seen as the sum of your abilities. While it is important to be in control of facts and possess know-how, being 'clever' is not enough for effective communications. The image of the doctor who lacks a bedside manner is an example of high-level knowledge undermined by poor interpersonal skills.

Outstanding communicators use their IQ skills to go far beyond just supporting their argument with facts and figures. IQ skills are crucial for information gathering in preparing your case, where you should:

- keep up to date with market, government policy, public sentiment and competitor developments;
- gather, probe and test information from a wide variety of sources;
- prepare thoroughly, spending time understanding the rational basis of the assignment and objectives you face in your communications;
- plan thoroughly for contingencies, preparing for any situations that might occur and cause difficulties;
- monitor situations carefully by maintaining a constant awareness of issues which may help or hinder progress.

In analysis of any communications challenge you face, your IQ skills will help you to:

- define the challenge, and help you establish specific objectives you need to achieve;
- think broadly and strategically, with an understanding of the issues and contexts you face;
- grasp the key facts of a situation by breaking information into component parts and identifying individual relationships between the different elements;
- evaluate actions in terms of their potential impact on overall objectives;
- identify potential outcomes of a situation, weighing up the positive and negative results of your decisions.

The Greek philosopher Aristotle observed the potent persuasion of Sophist professional orators in ancient Greece. A key facet to their skills was their use of what he called 'logos', the rationality of a message. Lessons from the Sophist orators in using logical proofs include:

- Deliver your message in a confident and authoritative manner.
- Get targets to argue against their own position.
- Back up your arguments with case studies and hard evidence.
- Share two-sided arguments with intelligent people, but refute counter-arguments.
- Have a consistent sliding scale of sequential requests, starting with low minor points of agreement and going on to higher-level key issues.

Jackie Le Fevre, a public relations specialist in the voluntary and community sectors, often finds campaigners overlook the need to base their campaigns on sound intelligence. They are keen to tell the world about their particular message, but assume everybody will automatically recognize the justice of their cause.

She recalls one campaign where community groups, angry with their local health authority at the withdrawal of GP services from a local surgery, automatically thought other stakeholders would instantly see the validity of their arguments and take up arms on their behalf:

> The residents were initially stunned when their appeals for help were not instantly accepted. The first thing I got them to do was conduct an in-depth questionnaire, which I helped them to produce. The survey findings, based on over 100 interviews, substantiated in a calm, factual way, using non-emotive intelligence, the issues and needs they had identified. Armed with this new ammunition they were listened to, attracted supporters and subsequently opened up the debate they so badly wanted to have.

Facts are truly powerful tools for persuasion. The world of financial public relations, for example, needs to base campaigns on accurate and credible intelligence. Andrew Mann, Investor Relations Manager, at BAE Systems, argues that getting the facts right is fundamental to doing his job effectively:

> The role of investor relations is based on explaining your company story to the financial community in terms that the recipient can understand and within the constraints of the regulatory frameworks. This can only be achieved by explaining facts and figures. There should be no element of 'spin doctoring' involved.

As respected Yorkshire journalist David Marsh observed, 'Facts are sacred.'

Task: putting it into practice

Review a recent unsuccessful communications activity. Did you prepare sufficiently? Did you do your homework? Did your thinking possess an inherent logic? Did you articulate the logic of your point of view? What action points can you identify to ensure future campaigns sufficiently harness logic and facts?

EMOTIONAL QUOTIENT (EQ)

Perceptions are more often based on emotions rather than facts. First labelled by Daniel Goleman in his *Emotional Intelligence* (1996), the emotional quotient (EQ) is defined as the ability to sense, understand and apply the power and acumen of emotions as a source of human energy, information, trust, creativity and influences.

Using the example again of doctors, if they harness their great medical knowledge with high EQ skills they can resource their IQ abilities in medical knowledge, coupled with the EQ insights to make a more holistic assessment of their patients' needs. This EQ ability would provide the necessary empathy to boost patients' emotional state and help them deal with their condition.

Your EQ skills enable you to establish the bigger picture of any situation. It helps you go beyond the obvious logical elements, by considering links and similarities between seemingly unrelated issues to distinguish between core issues and peripheral ones. Your EQ enables you to deal with ambiguity, to make positive use of the potential opportunities inherent in any situation.

Your EQ enables you to take responsibility and accept that mistakes are made – and be the first to admit your own mistakes. It helps you handle criticism well and learn from it, seeing it not as blame but rather as constructive feedback, offering a learning experience to gain from.

Your EQ skills enable you to foster openness and information sharing among your colleagues and peers when gathering information. You seek help from others when required, canvassing suggestions and options to create a culture of information sharing. Using your personal experiences helps you to understand problems. You ask questions around other people's own issues, and work to understand their motivation. Your EQ skills enable you to pick up on verbal and non-verbal cues in any communication.

In delivering communications you use your EQ skills to adapt communications to the needs of their audience, and to speak with conviction. Your EQ can enable you to act with confidence when communicating your message.

In dealing with people you consider the impact of an action on others by.

● demonstrating interest in others by working towards solutions of mutual benefit;
● showing respect, sympathy and sensitivity to individual needs and cultural differences by tolerating differing needs and viewpoints;
● understanding the objectives of all parties and keeping an open mind when others are expressing their views;
● behaving consistently with clear personal values and setting high goals and standards, where your actions are consistent with your values;
● providing advice and coaching to your colleagues; formally and informally acknowledging their contributions;

● using humour as a means of gelling relationships and fuelling team spirit.

Aristotle also recognized the importance of EQ skills in persuasion, although he labelled them 'ethos' – the credibility of the persuader – and 'pathos' – how to use appeals to the emotions (www.u.arizona. edu/~tkinney/pdf/handouts, one of many sources of information on Aristotle).

Reflecting on the significance of harnessing emotional intelligence in public relations communications, Jackie Le Fevre argues that in the community and voluntary sectors it is inconceivable to deliver effective communications unless communicators fully empathize with their target communities. Similarly in financial public relations, Andrew Mann of BAE Systems highlights the significance of having strong emotional quotient skills:

> In one-to-one briefings people buy people; do they believe what you say and trust you will deliver your promises? Body language, being able to read people's emotions and translate or adapt your information to their needs and feelings, are crucial to ensuring you get your message across.

Chapters 4, 5 and 6 will explore how you can harness different emotional qualities in shaping your messages.

Task: putting it into practice

Do you put yourself in the shoes of target audiences and try to look at the world from their view? Do you use emotional appeals in your communications? In what ways do you use humour in your communications? Do you use it appropriately? Could using humour help you be better understood? Does your humour get in the way of the communications?

VISION QUOTIENT

A vision can be likened to having a destination on your horizon which you intend to reach on your journey. The actual picture in your mind's eye might be very well defined, where you have a clear specific understanding, and possibly experience, of what the place you are heading for is like. Alternatively, it could be an imagined goal. If it is imagined, the more sensory detail you can imagine, the more the vision will be coherent and potentially attractive to you.

The role of vision can be anything in your life: from profound issues like what you are achieving with your life through to specific tasks such as how successful your next press release will be. The vision needs to be bigger than you, or where you are at present in relation to your task or life.

Outstanding public relations communicators possess a vision of a potential positive outcome to their communications challenges. Their vision provides a compelling image of a desirable and achievable future. There is a lot of truth in the management cliché, 'Vision – no leader leaves home without it.' Vision is crucial to success, whether it is running a country or organization, or issuing a press release; they all need a vision in order for the task to be fulfilled. If, for example you are producing a press release and you have a limited vision of its potential success, guess what the likely outcome will be? The more coherent and defined your goal, the more likely you are to achieve it. Oscar Hammerstein observed, 'If you don't have a dream, how are you going to make your dream come true?'

What you intend, you create. The fastest way to change how you feel about anything is to change what you are focusing on. You would not sit through a bad film twice, so why do it in your mind? A vision is essentially your mental map set in the future. Successful communicators set a goal and take immediate and massive action to deliver it.

Your vision quotient contains two elements. The first is the sense of a horizon of where you want to be. Second, this should ideally be underpinned by specific goals which are stepping stones to reaching the vision. Winning starts with beginning. As the comedian Woody Allen quipped, 'A key part of success is just showing up.' Set your communications goal and take immediate action to support it. It may be a cliché but the communications journey of a thousand miles begins with a single step. Begin it.

A useful tool for devising your vision is the acronym SMARTA, where your goal needs to be:

- **Specific** – it is focused to a clear-cut objective.
- **Measurable** – have a framework to evaluate it and define if it is successful.
- **Achievable** – there is a clear sense of a winning line.
- **Realistic** – it can be achieved with the resources available.
- **Time-based** – the plan is bound in a timeline of doing.
- **Awesome** – something provocative to throw into the mix, to overcome potential problems of playing things too safe. It provides a stretching goal to challenge any self-limiting boundaries.

When communication fails it is often down to a lack of clarity in both the vision and the goal. (Chapter 6 will examine how you can trigger your message to achieve change.) Lord Saatchi, the former Conservative

Party Chairman claimed his party lost the UK general election of May 2005 because 'I did not debunk the mirage of "professionalism" by which marketing, advertising, mailing, calls etc can outweigh the power of a simple vision' (Saatchi, 2005).

People have different thinking styles. A majority of people are visually biased in how they prefer to manage information. For them vision is quite literally a picture, an imagined image. However, you do not have to be visual to be able to envision. Others are auditory, where they prefer to process information by sound. Their vision will be sound-based. Tactile people are people who are most comfortable when there is an element of touch in their information gathering. They will develop a sense of feel for their vision. Do not turn your nose up at the power of smell. The nose is highly sensitive to different pheromones, while the stomach has as many nerve receptors as the brain.

Successful communicators who harness vision use positive thinking as a fuel for maintaining what is essentially a piece of imagination. The positive thinking exerts a feeling of making the vision feel alive, is based in a reality, and will be done.

There has been a massive growth industry in personal development texts, preaching the power of positive thinking. There is a danger that people can become positive thinking zombies, unstintingly observing and reacting that everything is positive, a bit like the character Dr Pangloss created by Voltaire, who irritatingly saw any disaster as for the best. Yet pessimism or scepticism can be good. It can provide a reality check on your actions. In managing any communications you need to know about realistic threats and challenges. If something is not working, or is threatening not to work, you want to be aware of these developments in good time. Yet if you are constantly pessimistic, the negativity could dampen, preclude or imprison potential good things. As the adage goes, there is no point being pessimistic, it probably won't work! The trick is to harness 'pit-stop pessimism' – use it as a quick reality check and then move on. Pessimism is unhelpful when it is made permanent – creating a mindset of 'thinking it will never happen' – or pervasive – where whatever we do, we think that it will never work.

Outstanding communicators think broadly beyond immediate issues, think ahead by using vision, and focus on the benefits of the future rather than the past. They show awareness of long-term benefits over short-term political issues. They maintain a positive outlook, look for positive outcomes and remain optimistic. They communicate messages of hope. Bertie Ahern, the Irish Taoiseach (prime minister) frequently used this technique during the numerous setbacks faced in establishing peace in Northern Ireland, where he reflected that 'Things will get worse before they get better.' Faced with being unable to find a positive in the short term, he resorted to a longer-term perspective.

> **Task: putting it into practice**
>
> The last press release you wrote, or last campaign you created – did you have a vision for its potential success? When entering negotiations or managing conflict, do you have a positive vision of a successful outcome to the situation?

ADVERSITY QUOTIENT (AQ)

Now matter how strong and potent your vision is, you will inevitably run into obstacles, potential barriers that prevent you from reaching where you want to be. The greatest skill of the communicator is not to give in. The pioneer of personal development texts, doctor and journalist Samuel Smiles, noted in his *Self-Help*, 'Looking at some of the more remarkable instances [of successful people], it might also be said that early encounters with difficulty and adverse circumstances were the necessary indispensable condition of success' (quoted in Lancaster, 1993).

A more recent example cited by the self-development guru Anthony Robbins in his conference presentations tells the story of actor Sylvester Stallone, who in his early days was turned down a thousand times by casting agents in New York. There were only 10 agents involved, but he was turned down again and again by the same agents.

Adversity quotient is the will to succeed, your resilience, the ability to bounce back, not be deterred in your quest. Everyone has setbacks; the successful communicator overcomes these. Outstanding communicators confront difficult people when necessary on difficult issues.

Key resources for your adversity state are:

- accountability;
- meaning;
- persistence;
- flexibility.

Accountability

Successful communicators are 100 per cent accountable. They inevitably face setbacks but make themselves 100 per cent accountable for dealing with their problems. Leading motivational speaker Steve McDermott regularly asks his audiences, 'What percentage of your life's success is down to you and what percentage is down to things you have no control over – such as luck, class, circumstances?' (I heard him at an event in

Hull in May 1998.) Among business executives he gets a figure usually of around 80 per cent down to them. His response is that it needs to be 100 per cent. Successful people have setbacks but make themselves completely accountable for doing something about them.

As part of an urban regeneration initiative I invited Steve to speak at an event for council estate representatives. In contrast to his business audiences the figure he got in response to his question was the complete opposite: these people felt just 20 per cent of their fortune was down to them. They felt they had very little, or no, control over their lives and their futures. Millions of pounds had been spent on bricks and mortar in the regeneration initiative, but nothing on the minds and attitudes of the people. This seriously undermines the sustainability of the regeneration investment: as soon as something goes wrong the people at the heart of it do not see themselves as accountable, or feel responsible for doing anything about it.

Marc Evans, a strategic communications consultant, always recalls the golden advice he received in his early career as a radio researcher: 'People never call you back. Always tell them you will call back, and do so on time.'

Meaning

In order to achieve any success a task must have meaning. The writer Douglas Adams in the last years of his life suffered from a major case of writer's block. He had secured a multi-million publishing deal yet the words for his book would not come to him. Adams had figured the number of words required for the book and even estimated a cash figure for each word. Having enjoyed success with his various *Hitchhiker's Guides to the Galaxy* books, he savoured a good lifestyle in California. He evidently was not driven or motivated by money. In his thinking he had actually given the commission of writing the new book a negative meaning, evidently prompting his writer's block. All of us have jobs that we have not got round to doing. More often than not, despite the many lame excuses for inactivity we come up with, the real reason is that the activity has no perceived clear or valued meaning for us.

The challenge for the successful communicator is to ascribe positive meaning to any task. During a creativity training course for a group of radio advertising creatives, one delegate recalled to me how he struggled to come up with ideas for a campaign to recruit special constables (unpaid volunteer police officers). The guy remembered the thought process going through his head: 'Why would anyone want to be an unpaid copper?' He had successfully created for himself negative meaning to the assignment – which provided a barrier to his normal creative flow. He could have reframed the brief as identifying a value which had personal meaning to him, such as: 'I want to live in a community where people can feel safe.' He then could have embarked on the job of generating ideas to address this task.

Persistence

There's no such thing as a guaranteed winning lottery ticket. Persistence usually pays (except for lottery tickets!). Every time you do something you learn from it and have the opportunity to find a way to do it better next time.

Even if faced with a rejection you should obtain positive sustenance from the experience. As black rights activist Derrick Bell (2002) advises, 'if they reject … then you must make their rejection your strength'. You need to hold fast to your passion, you cannot be a slave to someone else's game or agenda. The golfing cliché 'The harder you prepare, the luckier you seem to get' is as true in life as it is on the golf course.

Flexibility

Outstanding communicators combine the ability to take risks and also stick with things. They have the talent to know when to drop something and walk away. The more options and opportunities you have, the more flexibility you have at your disposal. Your AQ skills enable you to respond positively to changes or setbacks, where you remain calm and in control of your emotions. You manage pressure well, working productively in challenging situations by keeping your emotions under control and remaining emotionally stable.

John O'Grady has significant crisis public relations experience working for various utilities including National Grid Transco and Northern Gas Networks. O'Grady believes that at the heart of any successful management of a crisis is the adversity quotient of the individual:

> In times of a crisis the PR person has got to be able to stand up for themselves; you often have to take the lead, setting the agenda with the media and other stakeholders. Emotions are often running high and the temptation for some managers – even at a very senior level – is to keep their heads down, personally and corporately. If you are weak you will let yourself down, undermine any confidence the media may have in you, and also damage the reputation of your organization. You do need an inner toughness to see you through these situations. It's only when the crisis is over that you have the time to reflect and critically analyse your own performance. When the dust has settled, I find it useful to talk to the key contacts to get some feedback, good and bad.

Even in the world of consumer public relations, adversity quotient is a crucial skill underpinning success or failure. Mike Morgan is chief executive of UK consultancy Red, a firm which has won many, many awards for its creative solutions to consumer campaigns. Yet Mike puts bravery ahead of creativity as the reason for his team's success: 'Be brave, because half-hearted communication leads to oblivion. The most common cause of failure is compromising on clarity and strength of story in the face of demands to conform rigidly to core marketing messages.' He added:

> Advertising professionals have a touching faith in PR's ability to mesmerize media into carrying explicit 'above the line' copy in stories or broadcasts. In their world they 'buy' space and fill it with whatever they wish. In our world we have to 'win' space by meeting the media's need for content that comes with appropriate – as judged by the media – levels of branding and branded messages. The key is, the more integral you are to the story, the deeper the branding. 'Doing' gets you more than 'saying' is the general rule of thumb. There will be many times when you will need to be tough to deliver what you believe to be right.

Task: putting it into practice

Think back to any unsuccessful campaign. Did you give up too soon? Were there any positive lessons which could be reused in some way?

THE FOUR QS OVERVIEW IN COMMUNICATIONS: GETTING THE BALANCE RIGHT

You can achieve a high communications quotient as a result of effectively harnessing the different elements of the four Qs, and using the appropriate resource for the specific context and challenge you face. You will for example inevitably face setbacks in your communications where you could either give up, or use your adversity quotient to bounce back. Your vision quotient provides a sense of destination for defining and conceptualizing the mission and establishing a focus for where things are going. The interplay between IQ and EQ resource states provides a comprehensive source for content and analysis. By recognizing your different competencies you can draw upon different resources to provide the will to succeed to meet the communications challenge you face.

The trick in managing the four different Qs is to get the balance right. Greg Dyke, the former director general of the BBC, ruefully reflected on his battle with the British government over news reporting in the run-up to the Iraq war in 2004, that perhaps he had been over-combatative in his approach, spoiling for a fight over broadcasting independence which ultimately led to his resignation. He had over-used his adversity quotient in this instance (Dyke, 2004).

Which resource states are most helpful? Table 2.1 provides some suggestions.

Table 2.1 *Which resource states to use when*

Situation	Key resources to use
Research/factual story	Your IQ skills to analyse the significance, understand the subject matter and its context are the fundamental starting point for your communications in this situation. By relying too much on IQ, and failing to translate your expert knowledge to other less knowledgeable people, you can hinder your communications.
Human interest stories	Your EQ skills: your ability to empathize, get under the skin of your subject, understand what other people would be interested in on an emotional level are crucial for these opportunities.
Crisis situation	Your AQ skills – ability to cope with pressure, stand up and fight your corner if necessary, and bounce back from adversity are all critical in a crisis. Your VQ skills to look beyond the immediate problems and any short-term difficulties, to depict a future horizon to move towards, can also be helpful.
New campaign	Your VQ skills in being able to paint a new world, with the success of your campaign already envisaged in your mind, will help propel you and your colleagues forward in delivering communications.

Language

The language you use expresses information from you, but also can betray your inner thinking and also can predict how you are going to perform. The specific words you use can reinforce your mental maps to create self-fulfilling consequences in your subsequent behaviour. Persistent use of 'can't', mustn't', 'never' or 'no one' can create a self-determining mode of thought, a self-fulfilling prophecy. Conversely, using empowering words such as 'will' and 'can' creates a positive sense of purpose.

Excessive use of universals – all, every, never, always, no one, everyone – can also lead to over-use of generalizations and close the mind to those inevitable exceptions.

The rigid, inflexible mind

Having rigid, limiting mental models will hold back your communications – and your life. It can severely hamper your ability to achieve any form of empathy – the ability to put yourself in others' shoes – with your communications target. You can recognize if you are displaying the typical characteristics of an inflexible mind if you:

● insist your ideas are the only reality;
● have a narrow set of interests to ensure you ignore a lot of experiences;
● do not tolerate ambiguity and jump to conclusions as fast as possible;
● devise creative excuses to explain things away when things do not go as you planned;
● use lots of negative determining words in your language, such as 'never' and use many universals, like 'always';
● are quick to generalize;
● set up plenty of one-sided unfocused experiences to provide evidence of your ideas, or blame failures squarely on others and do not examine other possible factors;
● think solely in straight lines of cause and effect;
● are never curious and never update your beliefs in the light of experience.

Whenever you as a communicator are faced with limiting mental models, whether it is something within yourself or from someone else, here are four ways to challenge your mental map:

● Who says?
● So what?
● Why not?
● What evidence have you got?

Task: putting it into practice

Re-examine some of the language you have used in situations of conflict, negotiation or in managing a relationship. Did your language display a flexible or inflexible mind?

YOUR COMMUNICATIONS QUOTIENT AND YOUR PERSONAL BRAND

To help your intrapersonal skills you need to understand your 'brand' of thinking and how it is created by your differing strengths in the different quotient resources, coupled with your ability to get the right balance from them for the job in hand. By recognizing that your communications are made up of an interplay between the different quotients you can gain an intrapersonal insight into your own thinking. Is your thinking dominated by one quotient? Do you make insufficient use of certain quotients: does your thinking lack vision, intelligence, emotion or robustness with adversity?

By having a greater understanding of how you think, you can manage this dimension and the impact it has on your subsequent communications. You will also appreciate what characterizes your own brand of thinking.

Creative industries writer Richard Florida (2002) observed how a time traveller from 1900 would be amazed at the technological changes he or she would witness visiting a city of 1950, with the advent of the motor car and airplane being two obvious differences. The same time traveller moving on a further 50 years would recognize much that was familiar to him or her from the world of 1950, with just changes in the styling and look of cars, planes and buildings. What probably would surprise him or her most about the world of 2000 would be the sociological changes he or she would witness, such as the changing role of women in society, and greater racial equality.

What changes would the visitor to 2050 notice? Perhaps the next big change, in my own view, is that people will have far greater understanding of their own and other people's intrapersonal skills. A more formal understanding of what shapes and drives people's thoughts, behaviours and attitudes could be the striking difference between us and future generations. (As my daughter said to me when she was just 12 years old, 'Dad, I hate it when you use reverse psychology on me!' What will her children be saying?)

PR FUTURES DEBATE

Should PR practitioners play a central role in defining an organization's vision?

Should PR be the prime discipline for shaping an organization's thinking – or at least helping to diagnose its particular brand of thinking?

PERSONAL CHECKLIST

- Check your language – is it positive or negative?
- Are you managing your pessimism or scepticism? Are you making it permanent and pervasive?
- Reflect back on any successful/unsuccessful communications and consider the contribution made by your IQ, EQ, VQ and AQ.

PRELUDE TO CHAPTER 3

You communicate not just with words or gestures. You communicate integrity and trust not by words. You have a range of languages to convey your message. Your ears are your best friend.

3

You and your interpersonal skills

As a public relations communicator you are a bridge builder. Your bridge is between different people to provide communications, understanding and cooperation, which spans from using the mental map inside your head to engage with the mental maps inside other people's heads.

The word 'communication' is derived from the Latin *communicare* which means 'to share together', or literally 'to make common'. The communications challenge begins with your understanding of the needs of your audience. The phrase 'treat people as you would like to be treated yourself' is a useful tool for respecting other people's needs. A more pertinent phrase would be 'treat people as they would like to be treated', recognizing that their world view will inevitably be different from yours.

How do you bridge the self-talk in your head to make common ground with the outside world? You ultimately manifest and communicate your mental maps through your behaviours and language. Underlying these are:

● actions;
● strategies to achieve trust and integrity;
● body language;
● other dimensions to 'language';

- active listening;
- active presenting;
- assertiveness.

COMMUNICATING THROUGH ACTIONS

Your actions are a form of communication. Indeed, they are the ultimate form of communication. As the adage goes, listen to what I do rather than what I say. You are what you do, not what you say you are. Your behaviours will often express your inner views and feelings.

If someone was to do a major presentation, with a full colour brochure, PowerPoint display, movie images and adverts saying 'I am wonderful and kind,' you might well believe it. If you actually saw the person doing unnecessarily horrible things what would you believe: what you have read and been told about, or what you have witnessed in his or her deeds?

Great communicators recognize that their actions carry a message. They ensure they act the part accordingly. Sir Peter Parker, the former chairman of British Rail, used to carry in his briefcase a dustpan and brush whenever he used the train service. He would make a point of tidying up the toilet and other facilities if necessary after he had used them. He no doubt told his staff many times to take pride in their railway and do all they could to make it better. With his dustpan and brush he demonstrated, with far greater credibility, that he genuinely meant it.

I once had a critical debate with the director of Yorkshire Forward, the regional development agency, on its appointment of an agency based outside the region in Manchester to promote the Yorkshire region. One of the development agency's core messages was that Yorkshire was alive with creativity and innovation. Yet in its actions by going outside the region to buy creative services, it had acted incongruously, in my view. Actions speak louder than words.

COMMUNICATING WITH INTEGRITY

It was the American writer Emerson who reflected on a compatriot's lack of truthfulness: 'The louder he talked of his honour, the faster we counted our spoons' (quoted on www.transcendentalists.com/emerson_quotes. htm). If 'watch my lips' words alone cannot communicate sincerity, how can you communicate genuine integrity? True congruence in your communications occurs when you behave in accordance with your beliefs and values.

Arthur Page, the former head of public relations at American telecoms company AT&T, had a forthright definition of public relations: 'Tell the truth and prove it with action' (www.awpagesociety.com). Advertising guru Bill Bernbach echoed the sentiment when he cynically remarked, 'I've a great gimmick. Let's tell the truth.'

Integrity goes beyond honesty. Honesty is telling the truth, making your words conform to reality. Integrity is making your reality conform to your words. So you keep promises and fulfil expectations of you. One of the most important ways to manifest integrity is to be loyal to those who are not present. By doing this you build the trust of those present. Integrity means avoiding communication that is deceptive, or beneath the dignity of people.

Personal integrity generates trust. People can on the surface seek to understand, remember little things, keep their promises, clarify and fulfil expectations, but still fail to build reserves of trust if they are inwardly duplicitous. Trust can operate at a deeply profound level – would you trust this person with your life? It can also be engaged in very minor trans-actions – can you trust this person to do a particular job?

Key strategies to employ to build integrity include:

- Become genuinely interested in other people by having the belief and value that everyone has at least one thing interesting about them. (A good ice-breaking comment is, 'What I really like about you is ...'.)
- Make the other person feel important and do it sincerely.
- Try honestly to see things from the other person's point of view.
- Help the other person be happy about doing what you suggest.
- Have an abundance mentality and let others have your ideas, by not being precious about ownership of 'your' idea.
- Understand and visibly live out your values.

Being genuinely interested in other people is a quality David Yelland of Weber Shandwick admires of Richard Branson:

> One of the top skills needed by outstanding business leaders is the ability to be comfortable with the media. I know from my own experience that Richard Branson for example, is genuinely interested in dealing with journalists and unlike many of his contemporaries will take a call, even when I was a junior reporter.

The challenge is to be truly integrated into the interests and well-being of others around you. As Martin Luther King Jr in his concept of the 'inter-related mutuality of life' reflected, 'I cannot be who I ought to be until you are who you ought to be, and you cannot be who you ought to be until I am who I ought to be' (quoted in Bell, 2002). By seeing your own integrity as part of a bigger picture and also how other people's condition is instrumental in achieving your actualization, you can truly impart integrity.

ACHIEVING TRUST

The first goal in any communication is to establish trust. People buy trust first, products second. Trust is the extent a person is confident in, and willing to act on basis of, the words, actions and decisions of another.

Trust is generated by five core principles:

- competence – you need to be able to deliver what you say;
- reliability – you need to deliver your promises and do what you say;
- openness – there should be transparency in your dealings;
- equity – a sense of fairness between the parties;
- giving – if you give something you are demonstrating a commitment to the relationship.

Familiarity only breeds trust when people can form repetitive, stable relationships. The more casual and ephemeral the encounter, the harder it is to establish a track record.

Trust is a must-have for communications, yet the forces making trust more vital are the same forces destroying it. You live in an age where everything is moving faster and relationships more fleeting. In this context you do not have time to check out the background or validity of every potential encounter. This, paradoxically, is also an opportunity: once you have built trust, your contacts tend to be more loyal as a result.

Individuals or organizations downsize. They fail to keep in touch with people, or focus on stakeholders crucial for their immediate needs, and longer-term relationships get put to one side, or wither away. In this context trust is crucial. If you trust someone, you can quickly make a decision about whether to use or work with them. This is perhaps the key driver behind the growth of brands in modern-day communications: a brand provides a badge of trust. (This will be explored in greater detail in Chapter 5.)

Most organizations have large 'corporate distrust departments' spending their time checking on people. Do you have the equivalent in the way you view and communicate with the world? Low trust is a recipe for high-cost management and administration for business and for you. Low-trust behaviour encourages knowledge to be hoarded and ideas to be shared only formally. High-trust people bestow knowledge on one another to develop joint understandings. Trust and cooperation are vital to future work cultures. (People should take a leaf, or the leaf, out of the American company Nordstrom: its employee handbook is just one page long and says, 'Use your good judgement in all situations.')

Unlike the 'claquers' of early Italian operas, who were members of the audience paid to applaud their paymaster performers, people will do things for you not because they have to, nor because they hope it will do them good in the end, but because they genuinely want to. You cannot pay people to appreciate you or even worship you. You can only achieve this through building a relationship of trust.

Trust must have accountability. In trust relationships there is only one sanction: if the trust is broken then the relationship ends. Trust therefore can be tough. You have got to earn trust, be open with people and take people into your confidence. Equally you need to recognize that trust is like the topsoil on the earth's surface. If it is gone nothing can grow there.

You can overcome negative barriers caused by people failing to trust you or your message by:

- taking their negative belief to its logical conclusion;
- giving counter-examples to demonstrate potential credibility;
- identifying another belief which may have stronger potency for the situation;
- exploring a detail for building common ground;
- depicting a wider bigger picture which can create a common denominator.

(Chapters 5 and 6 will explore in greater detail the strategies and tactics for building trust in your messages.)

When discussing outcomes in a relationship underpinned by trust you need to:

- Define as far as possible the parameters of the relationship. What are the limits and boundaries of where you want the relationship to go, and what you would like both sides to gain from it?
- Envisage the goals and objectives in the relationship. What does everyone want to get out from the relationship?
- Establish the effects of non-achievement, identifying the consequences if the relationship fails to deliver its goals or objectives.
- Identify the available tangible and personal resources.
- Acknowledge the accountability everyone in the relationship has to each other, and make other people accountable for their responsibilities.

Trust needs to be tested regularly to establish if still appropriate and warranted. Closed inward-looking trust promotes stability and cohesion but is at odds with open, questioning trust promoting creativity and change.

Trust is the gel holding together the loose and the informal in a fast-moving world, where relationships are moving towards being flexible, adaptable and non-permanent.

John Drummond of Corporate Culture is a leading specialist in corporate social responsibility. He believes trust-related marketing is based on five key principles:

> You need authenticity – it's got to be believable and backed by company actions; you have got to offer personal benefit and present your product or service in the context of their life; you need to establish empathy, using language and images they can relate to; you need to make sure your timing is relevant to current media issues; and lastly you need to tap into their convictions, the beliefs they hold in their lives. Using all these dimensions can enable you to build trust.

Task: putting it into practice

Reflect on any situation where you were managing conflict, or negotiating with someone. How did you communicate with your actions? How did you demonstrate your integrity and what did you do to build trust?

BODY LANGUAGE

Although his research on body language has often been applied in an overly simplistic or indiscriminate manner, the research by psychologist Albert Mehrabian (1972) still offers insight, suggesting we obtain around 52 per cent of information about other people from their body language, 35 per cent from their tone of voice and only 7 per cent from the words they use.

There is no real-life equivalent to Pinocchio's nose to provide an unambiguous signal that someone is lying. Charlie Whelan, the former press secretary to Gordon Brown, the Chancellor of the Exchequer in the UK government, claimed however that he could read the body language of his former colleague Alistair Campbell, then press secretary to Tony Blair, the UK prime minister. Whelan felt it was possible to tell when Campbell was not telling the truth by reading his body language, or more precisely, by monitoring his habit of sniffing in a derisive manner: 'Every time he lies, he sniffs' claimed Whelan (Oborne and Walters, 2004: 214).

Regardless of watching out for tell-tale signs of sniffing, even the security services have no sure-fire way of testing for lies. A big lie is that 'lie detectors' work. There are nonetheless some signs that someone might be engaged in deception, including:

- higher vocal pitch;
- slower speech rate;
- longer pauses;
- large number of speech errors and hesitations;
- shorter response length to questions;
- decreased use of arms, hands, fingers, feet and legs;
- more indirect answers that do not specifically refer to the self.

Other elements in the way our bodies interact and communicate with others include the following.

Open/closed body language

We tend to exhibit 'closed' body language when we cross our arms and legs, and orientate ourselves away from the person we are speaking to. It can signal being closed to any new information we are receiving. It can mark our being agitated and a sense of unease with our immediate environment. (Note: you need to be careful to distinguish between underlying truths expressed through body language and the fact that for some people, or in some situations, this body posture might simply be more comfortable.)

'Open' body language, in contrast, displays uncrossed legs and arms, where we point our body to the person we are speaking to, and often make gestures involving displaying open palms. It reveals an openness to new stimuli and being at ease in our environment.

When communicating you should be receptive and sensitive of other people's body language, but also be aware of your own actions and the signals they are transmitting to your audience.

Posture

The way you use your body makes a fundamental statement about yourself. An aligned, erect posture communicates ease. Unfortunately poor posture is often based on outdated personal habits. You become used to habitual postures which although they might feel right to you, send out incongruous signals and messages to others.

Gesture

Gestures need to be natural and spontaneous. You should also avoid unnecessary gestures. Gestures should only be used to emphasize a point. Nervous gestures are best dealt with first by identifying them. Watching a video of yourself presenting is a useful way of seeing how you come across and your often unconscious use of gestures.

In international communications you need to ensure your kinesics (your communication through body motion) is not misunderstood. Even body language might need to be translated. Shaking your head in Europe means 'No'. In parts of India it means 'Yes', and in Japan it might not mean either, but just indicate that you are paying attention.

Eye contact

Eye contact with the person you are communicating with should ideally be established for around five seconds. It is an important and natural expression of your interest. If dealing with a group of people establish eye contact with 'rapport leaders', people in the audience who are potentially more responsive, quicker to build a positive relationship with you and whose response is likely to be ahead of others.

Voice

There is a rich variety of information from paralinguistics, the nonverbal parts of the spoken word such as speech rate, intensity, pitch, modulation and quality of voice. A person's voice can also provide indicators of his or her social class, education, where he or she is from, and his or her health and well-being.

Your voice can be used to add energy and interest to your communication. Try to use it to express your natural emotions. Use it as an instrument to enable your performance to achieve maximum impact. The volume of your voice can be varied: soft to emphasize gentleness, or louder to express urgency. Fundamentally, people need to hear what you have to say.

Voice projection needs good breathing as it drives the voice. If you are nervous this shows in quick, shallow breathing. Use a voice congruent with your words. If you want people to share feelings, speak slower. If you are painting a picture with your words, and want the audience to visualize an image, then speak faster.

A leading voice coach in the UK, Lorraine Forrest-Turner, advises anyone about to present before an audience to take a tip from the acting profession and do a vocal warm-up:

> Taking long deep breaths, stretching facial muscles and doing tongue twisters like 'Red lorry, yellow lorry' not only improve diction, they help settle nerves and get brain and mouth 'into gear'. The more difficult the tongue twister, the more primed you are for performance. If you can say 'three thick thugs set three thugs free' and the 'sixth sheik's sixth sheep's sick' three times through without tripping over your tongue, you'll sound more confident and more authoritative.

Nervous verbal gestures

If you start a talk with the statement: 'I am not used to public speaking,' guess what the audience will think of your abilities. The tactic is a vain effort to try to gain a sympathy vote from the audience. Inevitably it fails, as the fundamental point registered in the audience's mind is, 'If this person is not very good why is he or she taking up my valuable time and talking to me?'

Sound fillers like 'um' and 'err' also transmit the underlying message that at the very least you are nervous, and therefore impart a doubt about the validity of your speaking to the audience, or suggest you don't really know what you are talking about. The adage of 'Physician, heal thyself' comes to mind. Watching your own performance on video is a very useful way of finding out about how you really come across to other people. Once you identify how you use these negative, counter-productive audio cues, you should replace them with more powerful statements such as a clear sentence or even a pause. Use the power of silence. Learn the art of the pause.

Space

Your body language is also defined by the way you use the space around you. The physical space around you is a metaphor for the mental space you occupy. When giving a lecture try to avoid standing behind a lectern. This physically creates a barrier between you and your audience. The lectern can symbolize your comfort blanket, a prop for you to hold on to, yet it serves as a physical barrier between you and your audience. If you are able-bodied, walk around the area in front of your audience, using relaxed, confident strides.

Where possible minimize space between you and your audience to create close proximity and help you build rapport quicker and more effectively. I have been known to rearrange the furniture in rooms when at pitch meetings. (Once, when faced with a room where the tables were laid out to create a large open square space in the centre, I picked up my chair and put it in the middle of the open space to deliver my presentation from the centre of the room.) You can use different spaces within the area you are presenting to emphasize key elements of your message. If your presentation contains certain negative elements you can deliver these from one part of the room, then move across to another area for other positive messages.

Task: putting it into practice

Practise with a partner or using a mirror and analyse your body language. What is it saying?

OTHER LANGUAGES

You communicate through a wide range of different methods. The psychologist Howard Gardner (2000) identified how we each possess a wide repertoire of different communication languages, and we each tend to have a preferred style among these. By using different elements of your multiple intelligences you give greater depth and resonance in your communication, as well as meeting the specific language needs of individuals.

Table 3.1 *Forms of intelligence and communication*

Verbal/ linguistic	Think in words
Logical/mathematical	See patterns easily. Like abstract ideas. Like strategy games and logical puzzles. Work out sums easily in your head.
Visual/spatial	Think in images and pictures.
Musical	Often sing, hum or whistle to yourself. Have a good sense of rhythm.
Bodily/kinaesthetic	Remember through bodily sensations. Have 'gut feelings'.
Inter-personal	Understand people well, pick up on other people's feelings.
Intra-personal	High degree of self-awareness.
Naturalist	Strong connections with the natural world. Drawn to and fascinated by animals and their behaviour.
Existential	Concerned with 'ultimate issues' about life and death.
Moral	Concerned with rules, behaviours and attitudes governing the sanctity of life.

Recognition of and working with and through these different multiple intelligences provides you with an important shift in terms of your communications. Too often your formal education leads you to a recognition and reliance on only two to three of these intelligences. Have a look at the list in Table 3.1. Which did your formal education focus on?

DRESS

Sherlock Holmes, the great fictional detective, had the ability to interpret detailed and extensive knowledge from a cursory inspection: 'By a man's finger-nails, by his coat-sleeve, by his boot, by his trouser-knees, by the callosities of his forefinger and thumb, by his expression, by his shirt-cuffs – each of these things a man's calling is plainly revealed.' The first impression people have of you when meeting you is of your appearance. Your appearance is a form of communication, yet is the way you appear what you want to communicate?

Research shows that people make their initial judgements about you in under 10 seconds.

Ideally you want to dress for comfort, put others at ease, and wear something appropriate for the season, time of day or occasion. As a general rule it is better to be overdressed than underdressed, match colours and styles you like, and err on the side of caution.

President John F Kennedy reportedly used to wear two vests and two shirts on cold days. In outdoor events he would be the only man without an overcoat, making him appear virile and strong in contrast to his overcoat-wearing colleagues. On the way to the scaffold in 1649 Charles I wore two shirts, as he did not want to shiver from the cold and appear nervous to the watching crowd.

Kevin Taylor of Companycare Communications reflects on the impact of a decision he made to no longer wear a tie for business meetings:

> I think the point to get across is confidence. There is a certain confidence you give yourself and you exude when you don't feel the need to 'dress up' in order to impress. I still wear what I hope are decent suits, well-tailored double-cuff shirts with cufflinks because I like that style of shirt, and well-polished shoes etc, but I don't feel the need to put on a tie even if the people in the office I am going to dress formally. I am confident that I still look smart, and I feel confident ... and because I do not necessarily conform to an expected dress code, I carry that air of confidence with me in the meeting.
>
> Of course many of the IT sector clients I visit dress informally, and in those cases the ultra-smart suit and tie look can alienate you from the client. Simply not wearing a tie is sometimes all it takes to fit in and yet stand out.

The state of your shoes is always a good way to judge a person's character. Scuffed, unkempt shoes show someone who lacks attention to detail, or is good at putting on a front. Immaculate, pristine shoes reveal someone with a close attention to detail and organization. Someone with a brightly coloured UK shoe size 36 is a clown.

Task: putting it into practice

What do your clothes say about you? Is your dress style appropriate for your personal brand?

ACTIVE LISTENING

Note that I've put this section before sections on active speaking and presenting! Have you ever come across anyone with two tongues and one ear? People prefer to talk rather than listen. Listening is defined as the acquisition, processing and retention of information from other people's verbal and auditory communications. It might seem odd to regard listening as a skill because you think of it as a passive activity, yet it is a grossly underestimated and understated skill.

Your ears will never get you into trouble. You learn through listening. They who listen are in control. Let others talk first. People do not always care how much you know, but they know how much you care by the way you listen.

Listening is more demanding than talking. It demands total concentration. Words are spoken at between 90 to 200 words a minute, but you have a much faster speed of thought. This is why it is easy to be distracted while listening.

Hearing is one of the body's five senses, but listening is an art. It is a mistake to think you listen only with your ears. You actually listen with your mind, eyes, body and intuition. Unless you truly want to understand the other person you will never be able to listen. Respect of other people, and their right to say what they have to say, underpins the art of listening.

Any discussion is often however a listening war, a verbal battle of words. Instead of listening and absorbing what the other person has to say, you often mentally start to debate your own ideas in your own mind and come up with counter-arguments or criticisms. While doing this you can actually lose track of the real point the person is making. Recognizing that changing your mind is not a weakness but a quality of accepting new information and making new judgements on it is also fundamental to good listening. People may shut their minds – and ears – off in a conversation, otherwise they might have to confront a new reality and have to change their mind.

We often go fact hunting. Instead of listening for the main theme or general points in the argument, we concentrate on the detailed facts and can lose sight of the overall message.

There are different types of listeners:

- pretend listeners whose minds are elsewhere;
- limiting listeners, who only give limited attention, focus on specific comments or topics, and may distort or misinterpret other things you say;
- self-centred listeners, only concerned with their views and just looking for agreement to their world-view or position;
- active listeners, seeking to gain new information and insight, or using the opportunity to show respect to the other person.

The quest of active listening is to:

- focus specifically on any messages communicated;
- gain full, accurate insights into the other person's communication;
- critically evaluate what others are saying;
- monitor any nonverbal signs;
- convey interest, concern and attention to the other party;
- encourage a full, open and honest expression of information;
- develop an other-centred approach during interaction, where the other person is deemed by you to be important;
- reach shared and agreed understanding and acceptance about each of your goals and priorities.

To stimulate your own self-talk into listening you need to prime your brain by establishing the belief in your head that 'this person has something important to say', and ask:

- What point is the speaker making?
- What does it mean?
- How is this helpful?
- How can I use the information the speaker is giving me?
- What sense does it make?
- Am I getting the whole story?
- Are the points being backed up?
- Finally, how does this relate to what I already know?

You can demonstrate your listening support by nonverbal communications such as eye contact, or reinforcing gestures. It is important to withhold your evaluation of what you think until the speaker has finished. Listen for main ideas, concentrate on substance not style, fight off any distractions, and stifle any feelings of anger if you are feeling angry. Read the feelings between the lines. Ask questions for clarity. Wait for the person to finish, and do not interrupt. At the end of the dialogue paraphrase what you understand the person to have told you. This also shows to him or her that you have listened, and helps to avoid people repeating themselves.

David Morgan Rees is a very experienced public relations practitioner in the UK. He is also beginning to have some hearing problems. Reflecting on his situation, David said:

> I have to concentrate more now on what others are saying. As well as learn-ing how my ears work, I have to pay attention to the many techniques of listening actively and creatively. It's a salutary and humbling experience.
>
> If we are to be fully effective, well-adjusted PR people, as well as being generous with thanks and praise in our working relationships, we have a vital responsibility to listen and observe keenly. It's a way of creating under-standing, trust and confidence between people. Our own PR skills and experience are very dependent on how we interpret others' ideas, beliefs and behaviours. So often it's the odd, easily-missed word or expression which reveals everything.
>
> We in PR ought to seek opportunities to study and learn more about how other professionals listen. It would help us to study how, say, priests, medical consultants or police detectives have had to learn the techniques of not only asking the right questions but of listening to and observing the responses of their parishioners, patients or suspects. Organizations like the Samaritans, the RNIB and RNID and Relate have developed structures for *active* listening to help overcome others' personal problems, often assuaging misery and saving lives.

The power of listening is a crucial skill, recognized by Kate Nicholas in her work as publisher and formerly editor-in-chief of the UK trade magazine *PR Week*. This has given her the opportunity to meet many outstanding communicators working in public relations. Were there any key qualities that united them? She commented:

> Each one in their different ways was able to create a memorable impact when you dealt with them. The most impressive had such a highly sophisticated understanding of current affairs and business agenda that they would put many editors to shame. They were able to talk intelligently about the place that their organization and client held within this framework, rather than simply towing the company line. But perhaps the most memorable aspect about these greater communicators was their ability to listen, to gauge the climate of opinion and to engage in an intelligent two-way dialogue.

In discussions about the role of writers in society they are often described as 'truth tellers', capable of delivering profound insight about a reality. This is certainly a key skill for public relations professionals. It needs to be married however with a much wider remit and skill of being a 'truth listener', able to pick up the unpalatable, discordant or something everyone else is overlooking.

Task: putting it into practice

How good a listener are you? How good are you really? What ways could you improve?

ACTIVE PRESENTING

When presenting to any audience fundamental tips are:

- Believe you have a right to be here to talk in front of these people.
- You are going to give something to these people by being before them; people will gain from you in some way. This gives meaning to the job. (Remember, an expert is someone who knows marginally more than the audience, or can enable the audience to know more about itself.)
- Put yourself in the shoes of the audience. What do they want from this encounter with you? How are they feeling?
- Talk through your body. Deliver through your body language that you have a confidence to be in front of your audience, and that you are rising to the occasion to take full advantage of the opportunity. Smile through your eyes.
- Be enthusiastic. If you are not enthused by your subject, how do you expect the audience to be?
- Watch the audience; what is their mood? Are they engaged?

If you need to achieve dominance in an encounter you can use a number of different communications tactics including:

- speaking in a louder voice;
- talking for longer;
- choosing a focal point in a room to speak from;
- standing in a raised position;
- sitting behind a desk;
- being at the head of a table;

- having a more impressive chair;
- engaging in interrupting;
- looking while speaking and using long glances.

An apocryphal survey revealed that people listed public speaking as their biggest fear, ahead of death in fourth place. (On occasions I have succeeded in combining the two by 'dying' in front of an audience!) When making a speech do not just deliver a script. People want to hear you speak, not read. Also avoid memorizing a speech. If you forget the words it can lead to a disastrous performance. At the outset make specific references to your situation, your hosts, or something that has previously been said. This overcomes the perception that you are working from a script, emphasizes you are also at ease talking to the audience, and bridges your contribution to the situation. If you use humour it is best to direct it at yourself; and make sure your presentation has a beginning, middle, and end.

Try to build rapport with the audience by getting them to do something physical together, such as standing up, shaking hands, raising their hands, laughing or changing position. Always finish on a high. Unless the subject is inappropriate, follow the old showbiz adage: 'Send them home happy.'

Sue Johansson of the Yorkshire Event Company has worked with, and witnessed, many of the leading presenters on the business lecture circuit. Her view on the difference between 'good' and 'not so good' presenters is down to some key issues: 'The great speakers are not necessarily the most eloquent, or know the best stories and jokes. The "best" enjoy what they are doing, speak from the heart and truly believe what they are saying.'

Task: putting it into practice

What different ways could you improve your presentations? Devise an action plan based on the key points identified in this book.

ASSERTIVENESS

Getting your way in communication is not just about having your say. Assertiveness is about standing up for yourself and your position in a way that does not violate the rights of another person. It is about expressing your feelings and opinions honestly and directly. It is quite distinct from aggressiveness, which violates the rights of other people by humiliating or threatening them.

As a public relations practitioner you need to manage your assertiveness by being honest about your own feelings and being clear, specific, and direct in what you say. If necessary, seek clarification if you are uncertain about something.

When giving criticism seek solutions rather than commenting on the personality traits of the other people involved in the situation. When things go wrong address the issues of the situation, not the people. Seek and ask for inputs and insights from others to solve any common problems you face. Avoid emotional labels, and give pointed and specific feedback. Do not just say, 'This is lousy.' Instead, say something like, 'This is not meeting the brief or specification.'

Assertiveness is not just about dealing with negative situations. When there is something positive to say, say it, and respond to positive feelings expressed by others. Be on a mission to give genuine compliments, and accept compliments gracefully. Self-deprecation by admitting mistakes or personal shortcomings can help make others feel more at ease. Make it your responsibility to initiate and sustain interaction.

Although there are many different techniques used in developing assertive behaviour, some key tactics to employ when dealing with a difficult situation include:

● Demonstrate you understand a situation by summarizing the facts.
● Indicate your feelings towards the situation and how it is impacting on you.
● State your requirements from a situation with your reasons and identify the benefits to other people from cooperating with your view.

Using the above formula enables you to confront other people without being aggressive. The emphasis is on seeking positive outcomes for both parties. By using assertive skills you can avoid others taking advantage of you. It enables you to disagree constructively and manage negative or conflict situations in any public relations campaign.

Through assertiveness you can:

● make reasonable requests;
● refuse unwanted/unreasonable requests;
● ask others to change their behaviour;
● give personal opinions, even if unpopular;
● express disagreement or negative feelings;
● respond to criticism.

Assertiveness helps avoid poisonous undercurrents building up in relationships, sustains your own self-esteem, and negates much needless worry or stress as well as being a valuable communications tool.

Reflecting on her work in local government public relations, Pat Gaudin, a leading professional in the CIPR's Local Government Group, recognizes assertiveness as a crucial skill for effective survival in a politically charged arena:

> As a professional communicator you have to be assertive to get your point across and make other people feel you are not putting them down. On the contrary, you often have to give them confidence in pursuing a particular line. Keeping politicians happy without compromising your integrity as a public official can be a challenging balancing act. Being strong, without being overbearing, marks out the great manager of public communications.

PR FUTURES DEBATE

Who is in charge of 'organizational trust' in your organization?
Who monitors 'integrity' within the organization?
Should these be the responsibility of public relations practitioners?

PERSONAL CHECKLIST

- Have you seen yourself when you communicate? What gestures, postures, and nervous signals are you transmitting?
- Do you look people in the eye when talking to them?(Do check on cultural differences: in some societies it is considered bad manners to look someone in the eye.)
- How can you improve the listening skills of your colleagues?

PRELUDE TO CHAPTER 4

Find out about how you shape messages and how memes are the currency for exchanging ideas. Discover how memes have the ability to live on and develop their own momentum beyond the original communicator. Perception is reality, and you shape your perceptions through paradigms, or 'boxes'; you relate to the world through same-box, small-box or big-box thinking. Discover how by being flexible in your thinking you can secure significant advantage in your communications. Learn that ultimately all ideas are contained in three-dimensional boxes called paramemes.

There are lessons to be learnt from trashy pop songs which you cannot get out of your head.

4

Creating messages, memes and 'spinning'

Examining the very fundamentals of how communications work can transform your performance as a communicator. Understanding the mechanisms of how communications are transmitted will help you shape and mould your messages more effectively, as well give you a valuable insight into what underpins the increasingly important areas of viral marketing or 'sneeze communications'.

THE MEME

Humankind has come a long way since our ancestors lived in caves. As well as cave painting they discovered the ability to harness fire and make stone tools. They also unleashed a far more powerful tool – the ability to store and share experiences, knowledge and know-how. The biologist Professor Richard Dawkins in his seminal work *The Selfish Gene* (1976) investigated how humankind developed through its genetic inheritance but also by its ability to transmit cultural information from one individual to another, between different groups and through different generations.

Dawkins coined the word 'meme' to describe the vehicle for how the data of ideas and information are packaged and possess a dynamic to potentially spread their message beyond one individual to the wider world. Communication studies typically work within the paradigm that information is transmitted between a communicator and his or her audience. What these studies crucially overlook is the ability of the information itself to have its own self-generating momentum, an ability to replicate, to live on beyond the original communication.

A meme acts like an invisible currency, enabling effective exchange and trade of information between individuals. Memes are the communication equivalent of what biochemical genes are to DNA. In the same way that genes provide biologists with a framework and tool for greater understanding of living things, the communicator can similarly gain insight into how to communicate effectively by understanding how memes work. If you can understand how information is retained and transmitted it provides the fundamental insight into how the communications process works, and importantly, how you can use it to transform your communications in any public relations activities.

Dawkins uses the examples of how people learn the song 'Happy Birthday', and how you probably know the story about the American woman who tried to dry her pet poodle in a microwave (an alleged urban myth) to show how memes work. While your brain has been accommodating 'Happy Birthday', the poodle myth and any other knowledge, you have also seemingly ignored or discarded vast amounts of other information to which you were exposed. You do not remember going on a 'Happy Birthday' training course, or someone formally teaching you the lyric. You were exposed to the information through seeing, hearing or reading about it. You then retained what you perceived as the details of the song or story, and subsequently relayed them, both deliberately and inadvertently, to other people.

Both 'Happy Birthday' and the urban myth of the heated poodle are memes. They constitute a body of information and ideas circulated well beyond their original transmission. Everyone uses memes, albeit mainly at an unconsciously competent level (they do it without thinking about it). The ability to successfully create and harness effective memes, and meme-friendly messages, is crucial to successful communications.

So what exactly is a meme? As characterized by Dawkins, it has three distinct elements. First, it must have some form of longevity to enable it to live long enough to be transmitted in some way to a third party. A brilliant flash of inspiration is not a meme unless it survives long enough for you to remember, record and transmit it to another in some way.

Second, a meme must have coherence. Only the 'best' memes manage to implant themselves in other people's consciousness. 'Best' is defined as the ability to replicate itself. How does the data appear evident, and how does it fit into your wider belief system? A meme which is internally consistent and does not contradict other beliefs you hold is more like to be structurally sound, and able to replicate itself.

The lack of this coherence would preclude the third quality of a meme, being copyable. A meme's copyability enables other people to make their own copy of the information, giving them the facility to absorb, retain, create and possibly pass on. This copying process does not always produce an exact copy of the original information.

Table 4.1 compares the characteristics of a meme with a press release.

Table 4.1 *Memes and press releases*

Meme characteristic	Press release
Longevity	Your press release will be reproduced either on paper or electronically, enabling the recipients to keep it as long as they wish. The sheer deluge of information received by a journalist and the temptation to delete your email without reading it might prevent the message getting through.
Coherence	Your news story has to be readily digestible by a journalist, often within a few seconds; if not, it is likely to be discarded. If your message is hard to grasp or to comprehend readily it will fail to replicate.
Copyability	If well written your press release could be used with the minimum of changes, making it more likely that it will be retained by the journalist and its contents replicated for use in his or her medium.

The more coherent and copyable you can make your message, the more likely it will be replicated. Once you propel your meme into the outside world you lose direct control over it. The more you can do at the outset to make your meme as robust as possible, the greater its chances for survival.

When UK telephone directory services were opened up to competition, the American firm InfoNXX.Inc paid £2 million for the number 118 118.

The UK public relations director for the company, William Ostrom, takes up the story:

> Although we were dismissed as mad for paying such a vast sum just for the number, we were convinced that in a crowded marketplace its memorability would be crucial. Even with 118 118, we also realized our campaign would need a strong personality working with great simplicity at every possible level and channel to create a nationwide viral effect for 118 118. It worked. The British public adopted and copied the style of the 118 twins, and made 'got your number' the popular catch phrase of the year. Our reward was making an unknown new entrant the market leader in less than a year.

Dawkins relates how the traditional song 'Auld Lang Syne' has mutated in its retelling. In its original version Robert Burns wrote the refrain as 'For auld lang syne', whereas it is now universally sung as 'For the sake of Auld Lang Syne'. Presumably the 'correct' words were sung initially, but 'For the sake of …' was evidently easier to sing and remember. Rather like the party game of Chinese whispers, through telling and retelling (or singing and resinging), the original has been slightly remoulded. It has grown beyond its original specific information into a version that, if it is to survive, must be readily coherent and copyable.

Something similar happened to me when I was speaking at a conference. The description of my talk supplied to the organizers included a reference to 'how we communicate by creating messages – or memes'. Much to my surprise, and with a rather delicious sense of irony, the publicity materials contained an amended text which read 'how we communicate by creating messages – or *memos*' (my emphasis). The word 'meme' had ironically failed to survive, or replicate. A new meme, the concept of communicating by 'memos', was inadvertently created!

The word 'memes' is itself not an efficient meme. There is a tendency for people to struggle with its pronunciation. I have witnessed a multitude of variations from 'mem-es', 'memms', and even 'mimos', rather than the supposed intention by Dawkins that the word 'memes' should sound like the word 'genes'.

All cultural products, including all content generated by public relations professionals, including press releases, speeches, soundbites, brochures, jingles, catchphrases, brand identities and websites, are ultimately memes. Their effectiveness depends on the ability to survive sufficiently long enough: on whether they are coherent, can be copied, reproduced and retained by a third party. Rather like a software virus, thought contagions proliferate by effectively programming for their own transmission.

Memes are often confused with the concepts of ideas or thoughts. Both are cognitive structures, but an idea is not a self-replicating entity. Nor are memes just words which are absolutes such as 'red', 'straight', 'hot' or 'cold' (although the concepts of 'red as a beetroot', 'straight as a die', 'hot as hell' and 'cold as ice' are memes). Memes are a combination of elements that form themselves into a distinct memorable unit, such as the ideas of 'wheel', 'wearing clothes', 'letters', 'calendar', *'Hamlet'*, 'the latest fashion', *'the Teletubbies'*, and 'post-modernism'.

When you send out a press release you are seeking to propel a meme into the outside world – a new combination of elements, with the aim of getting this new information registered and recognized in the minds of others. Having this insight can transform the way you approach writing a press release. Instead of thinking of how you best summarize the information available to you, you should consider in what way you can create a memorable message to enable others subsequently to pass it on. (This dimension is also investigated in Chapter 7 on word of mouth marketing.)

Alastair Campbell, the former adviser to British prime minister Tony Blair, has an outstanding reputation for managing messages in communications. An example of his skill was seen during the Kosovo war in 1999. Visiting a NATO media briefing in Washington, Campbell witnessed a rambling 25-minute statement from Jamie Shea, the NATO press office spokesperson, followed by 15 minutes from a NATO general. Observing the performance, Campbell told a colleague, 'They are saying too many different things.' His advice was to identify the top line message of the day – the story to be the headlines in the media – and identify how you want the story to be. The following day Shea delivered a short five-minute statement with a clear message. Campbell was effectively defining the memes of the story, making them clear, coherent and copyable, for the message to survive and be passed on by the media in as near to the original version as possible (Oborne and Walters, 2004).

Task: putting it into practice

Revisit any recent communication you have produced. How meme-friendly is it? Identify the memes within it. Rewrite it to make it meme-friendly.

Memes propagate by leaping from brain to brain via imitation. If the idea catches on, it propagates itself. The human language, first acted, then spoken and later written, is the principal medium of cultural transmission, creating what can be labelled the 'infosphere' in which cultural activity occurs. Memes are invisible and carried by meme vehicles – pictures, books, leaflets, press releases, sayings, tools, buildings and other tools that bridge different people.

In the same way as your biological genes can achieve immortality by being copied and replicated through your descendants, memes live on beyond the original communicator. Our society for example has a few contemporary papyrus fragments of Plato's *Republic*. Its philosophical teachings are not kept alive by these relics, but from the millions of copies (whether as books, discussions or in any other medium) that keep its meme circulated.

There is no necessary connection between a meme's replicative power, its 'fitness' from its own point of view, and its contribution to your personal fitness or interests. The first rule of memes, as for genes, is that their replication is not necessary for the good of anything. The replicators that flourish are good at replicating, for whatever reason. Although most memes replicate with the originators' conscious approval, presumably because of their perceived value of the benefit they can bring them, some memes might manipulate people into replicating them in spite of their judging them useless or ugly, or even dangerous to their health and welfare.

You might not like the following pop songs but there is every chance you will know the tune and a line or two of them: the 'Crazy Frog' tune, 'Agadoo' and 'Supercalifragilisticexpialidocious' from the film *Mary Poppins*. Many people find they cannot shift out of their head the most irritating jingle-like quality they possess. (Sorry for respreading these memes: one of these tunes is probably in the front of your mind now, and your day is ruined!) You do not want to know these songs but their inherent strength as memes – their memorability, copyability and ease of passing on – means they survive in spite of your individual rational judgement and objections to them.

The 'conspiracy theory' meme is an example of a meme with a built-in response to any objection that there is no evidence of a conspiracy existing. The person supporting the meme can retort, 'Of course there isn't any overt evidence, that's how powerful the conspiracy is!' The meme will persist quite independently of any 'truth'. Witness the pervasiveness of the theory that the moon landings were a hoax. Conspiracy theories still abound despite the facts that the Apollo moon missions involved several thousand people – which would have made it difficult to maintain a conspiracy of silence over any hoax – and that if there had been any hint at the time (during the Cold War) that the mission was a fraud, the Soviet Union would surely have taken the opportunity to capitalize on it.

Specific 'hoax' evidence has been debunked. There is no wind on the moon, so how did the American flag flutter in the film images? It was evidently a vibration from the aluminium poles the flag was mounted on. There are divergent shadows on the moon surface in the mission's photographs; but shadows are not parallel on earth and can be distorted by variations in surfaces. However the meme still survives formally on conspiracy websites and alternative publications, and as a meme in many people's minds. Its content ranges from broad awareness of the existence of a conspiracy theory, through to knowing some of the specific evidence used to support the hoax claims, and to believing them and actively transmitting them.

Memes are the currency of communication, enabling ideas to be conveyed from one person to another, and another. Crucial questions you need to address in your communications to make your message meme-friendly are:

- How coherent and easily understandable is your message?
- How easy is it for someone else to relay the message to another person? (Ask yourself what is the phrase, the key detail someone can pass on to another person, after he or she has received your communication, such as a press release.)
- How can your communication make itself replicable without your involvement and gain further coverage?

One of the leading thinkers in marketing communications, Robin Wight, co-chairman of London-based branding agency wcrs, reflects on changes he is witnessing:

> Advertising has lost its role as a maker of 30-second commercials which then act as the prime launcher for a brand message. Instead, communicators have got to create new prime launch vehicles to deliver and spread their memes. This will need to engage and harness the full range of marketing communications tools – PR, direct marketing and ambient to name a few.

Emphasizing the significance for communicators in understanding how memes work and how they should harness them in their work, he added, 'I just hope my competitors keep ignoring memes – if they don't catch on to them, they will be left behind!'

Task: putting it into practice

Next time you receive any communication material, assess how you received it, and what are its meme-friendly qualities. What are the memorable features of these new messages and how easily can they be passed on? Review a copy of a newspaper and identify the memes within it.

(Chapters 5 and 6 examine how communicators can shape the elements of a meme to improve the effectiveness of their communication.)

If memes provide the currency for communication, what are the elements that provide the building blocks for how we actually create memes and communications?

CREATING PARADIGMS AND THE ART OF 'SPINNING'

Perception is reality. Chapter 1 highlighted how by creating our own individual mental maps of the world each of us subsequently views the world in a unique way. You see the world through perceptions. When you communicate you are building bridges between your perception of a reality, or mental map, and other people's perceptions, or mental maps.

Try this simple test with a group of friends or colleagues. By yourselves, without conferring, write down the first five words you associate with the following words:

Car
Red
Chocolate

Now compare the words each of you have written, and count how many words are exactly the same in all your lists. (If you do have the same words, check to see if they are in the same order, or written in capitals or lower case.) I have done this exercise with hundreds of groups, and have never had a group that all wrote down the same five words. (The nearest I came was a group of Nigerian delegates who all had the word 'cacoa' – one of their country's prime export products.)

The reason people use different words, even with apparently relatively simple concepts such as 'car', 'red' and 'chocolate', is that they all mean different things to different people. You perceive the world, every object within it, though a unique picture frame shaped by your values, beliefs, experiences and connections. This picture frame is called a 'frame' or a paradigm.

'Paradigm' tends to be used to describe a frame of reference shaping how you perceive the world. The term is commonly used to describe a general mind state. This book will use a much narrower definition of the term 'paradigm' as meaning the boundaries of a perception.

The good news about paradigms is that they act as a crucial filter, providing you with a form of cognitive shorthand, a short cut to manage the complexity of information in the world around you. To use again the analogy of your brain as a sponge that soaks up all the information around it, without paradigms your brain could not manage the vast deluge of information available to it. It cannot handle the scale and complexity of huge amounts of data and then make effective use of it.

Think how many pixels a computer image contains. (A typical photograph can contain over a million individual pixels.) If you see something in your environment, it is far easier to decode the information as 'This is a picture of a dog' than to try to register and record the individual million pixels. The image of the dog is rendered meaningful by your assumption, which are on the lines of, 'This looks like other dogs I have seen before and it appears to accord with what I define as a dog. I also have a host of attendant feelings and emotions about this image.' Paradigms are made up from assumptions. In turn they create a set of further unconscious assumptions through which we deal with the world.

The bad news about paradigms is that they operate like a virtual reality headset, determining your focus, and setting limits to your vision of the world around you. Paradigms act as invisible boundaries, a prison cell, within which you seek to solve problems and provide answers, limiting and confining your thinking, as well as defining your available options.

Paradigms provide the equivalent of a pair of spectacles enabling you to see the world around you. They also determine the stage set of your mental maps. They shape what you perceive as the environment around you, providing the stage for your performance in this world.

Paradigms have been described as picture frames. The picture frame is created by assumptions. The most powerful analytical tool you have is the simple question, 'What assumptions are we making here?' By posing this question you can challenge the paradigm that is dictating how others perceive a situation. When I was a young public relations officer working in local government, I often used to get annoyed when a council department would ask me to write a press release on a scheme where the details were set in stone, and there was no scope to change any element of it. If I had been involved earlier, I used to think, I could have suggested changes to give the project far greater public relations potential. I little realized at the time that I was actually seeking to change the paradigm of the situation.

The picture frame of a paradigm is like a box – which led to the concept of 'outside the box' thinking. This is used to describe something unusual or radically different, or a new way of doing things. The idea is that a new radical activity is outside the box of existing thinking. Actually there is no such thing as 'outside the box' thinking. Ultimately everything exists within a paradigm, a box. The best we can do is to create a bigger box for our thinking. Your new idea might extend, or even tear down, the boundaries of the original paradigm. All you have created, however, is a bigger box, a new paradigm containing your new idea and subsuming the original one. Someone might later devise an even bigger box of thinking to further subsume your original paradigm.

When devising your communication you have three strategies for managing your perceptions and those of the target audience:

- **same-box thinking**: operating within the existing paradigms, where your message and content are within the confines of existing communication;
- **bigger-box thinking**: breaking down and going beyond the boundaries of the original paradigm to provide messages and content on a bigger scale;
- **smaller-box thinking**: changing an element or niche, or focusing on one smaller part of the existing paradigm.

Examples of bigger-box thinking

In 1966 the French President General Charles de Gaulle demanded that all US troops be immediately removed from French soil. With incisive speed of thought the US Secretary of State Dean Rusk politely replied: 'Would that include the ones buried in the military cemeteries, mon General?' (lbjlib.utexas.edu/Johnson/archives.hom/oralhistroy.hom/rusk/rusk04. pdf). De Gaulle was operating within the paradigm of the existing relationships between the countries and the current military reality. Rusk created a bigger paradigm by drawing on reference to the earlier military help given by the United States, and an inference about the moral debt still owed for the liberation of France in earlier wars.

The Beatles drummer Ringo Starr was once faced with a difficult question at the height of the group's fame in the mid-1960s: 'Are you a mod or a rocker?' If he had given either answer, he would have alienated large sections of their fan base. His answer was: 'Neither, I'm a mocker.' He astutely sidestepped the issue by refusing to answer the question solely within the two paradigms of 'mods' and 'rockers' given to him by the journalist. Instead, he created a bigger new paradigm of a whimsical concept, a 'mocker' (quoted in the film *A Hard Day's Night*, 1964).

Part of the success behind the bid by London to host the 2012 Olympic Games was down to bigger box thinking. Film maker Daryl Goodrich described the thinking behind his acclaimed bid video:

> I was handed the opening lines of a script. It said before there is an Olympic champion there has to be eight finalists; before there is a final there have to be 64 Olympians; before that there have to be 202 national champions; before that thousands of athletes; and before that millions of children must be inspired. We built it from there.

> (quoted in the *Sunday Times*, 10 July 2005)

Each successive stage was using a bigger-box paradigm to provide a context, leading ultimately to a message of inspiring the next generation of athletes.

Some problems with communicating bigger-box thinking solutions are:

- You can over dilute your message appealing to too broad a subject rather than the specifics of the job at hand.
- If you are creating something new you need an infrastructure to make it happen. It is like the joke about the man who invented the telephone: who did he ring? By creating a new entity you need supporting mechanisms to make it happen.
- There also tend to be groups whose interests might be undermined in any major paradigm changes. They may present a powerful voice defending their vested interest to prevent or hinder the success of any new paradigm.
- The situation might require an instant and immediate response.

Task: putting it into practice

What examples of bigger-box thinking can you identify in your own communications? What new examples of bigger-box thinking can you create in your next communications challenge?

Examples of smaller-box thinking

Think of any change where an aspect has been changed or altered. The fundamental host paradigm is still present. Only a small part has been changed. By changing one small element you can achieve added value. It might be identifying a niche audience in your communications, or changing the colour of your leaflet or logo.

Smaller-box thinking can be a quick win for injecting new life into an established campaign. Because it operates within established practice it is easier to implement and usually does not require significant additional resource. Table 4.2 gives some specific examples of smaller-box thinking to generate added value in everyday public relations practice.

Table 4.2 *Smaller-box thinking*

Item	Smaller-box thinking
Audience	Target a niche group, or individuals within your already identified audiences
Timing	Change the timing of an existing activity
Print item	Change the colour, size or shape
Brand	Create a sub-brand
Channel	Identify a more specific way of reaching your audience through an existing communications channel (for example, using an advertising insert into a publication you are already using for media relations purposes)
Metaphor	Change or introduce a new metaphor in your communications (see Chapter 6)

Task: putting it into practice

What examples of smaller-box thinking can you identify in your own communications? What new examples of smaller-box thinking can you create in your next communications challenge?

BEING FLEXIBLE IN THE DIFFERENT 'BOXES' YOU USE

In the same way that memes provide a tool for understanding how you communicate, paradigms similarly provide a model for understanding how you shape and mould your perceptions. By understanding how paradigms operate, the effective communicator can manage them to achieve greater results. By adopting a metaposition, a helicopter view, above and beyond the situation, the communicator has the ability to jump outside the boxes limiting other people's perceptions. The flexible thinker can also reflect on and manipulate the relationship with boxes to achieve added value.

The challenge for successful communications is to adopt flexible thinking to manage paradigms, so as not to be bound or constrained by what might hold others back. By effective redefining on a meta level, or making a minor adjustment to a mindset, you can leverage significant communication advantage. Below are examples of how flexible use of paradigms delivered great added value in communications. When faced with a challenge do not meet it head on, but use bigger-box or smaller-box thinking to gain new perspectives.

My daughter Charlotte was just two years old when she felt tired while out walking with her grandfather and asked him to carry her. Believing her capable of walking further, he declined. After two or three failed requests she changed her question. 'Gramps, can I have a cuddle?' She succeeded in being carried on her walk. (Her repertoire at the time also included 'I need sweets!')

Charlotte was also successful in demonstrating how by changing the paradigm in her communications she could successfully achieve her objectives. The young child had successfully 'spun' her communications, moving the paradigm from providing the need for physical support to exploiting an emotional appeal to a grandfather who would not want to turn down a request to cuddle his grandchild.

The term 'spin doctor' – or as Welsh politician Rhodri Morgan puts it, 'master of rotational medicine' (Pitcher, 2003) – is believed to have originated in the United States from baseball, when its first recorded use was by Saul Bellow in his 1977 Jefferson Lectures (Oborne and Walters, 2004). The *Concise Oxford Dictionary* defines the term as 'a political spokesperson employed to give a favourable interpretation of events to the media'. It has come to be seen as a pejorative term, laden with implicit abuse, implying someone being untruthful, deceitful and desiring to manipulate perceptions. The dilemma of ethical debate on the question of 'spinning' is highlighted by the rather cynical industry adage: 'What is the difference between unethical and ethical advertising? Unethical advertising uses falsehoods to deceive the public; ethical advertising uses truth to deceive the public.'

There has been a lot of nonsense spoken about how we live in an 'age of spin'. Manipulating paradigms, as demonstrated by a two-year-old girl, or in any study of political life through the centuries, is an inherent element in communications. If two people were to view a glass that was 50 per cent filled with water, one would be likely to say 'The glass is half full' while the other person, with equally validity, could observe that 'The glass is half empty.' However, both might experience some anxiety in judging that the glass is 'half' anything, since most people cannot judge quantities with such precision. (See Chapter 6 on dissonance.) 'Spinning' is therefore inherently rooted in any communication. This is not to say, however, that disreputable activity in the form of knowingly lying or misleading can be excused. (For a more extensive review of ethical questions in communications the reader is referred to *Ethics in Public Relations* (Parsons, 2004).)

In order to manage the effectiveness of your communications you need to understand the mechanics underpinning the tactics of 'spinning', or managing the paradigms of your message. These include the following.

Minimizing the significance

This is done by placing the paradigm in the context of a bigger paradigm. You are highlighting that your message is a small box within a bigger box issue. The singer George Michael was arrested in 1998 at a public lavatory in Beverly Hills, California for 'lewd behaviour'. He pleaded guilty and received a fine and a community service order. This would have been the end of a career for many other stars, but Michael's popularity actually rose. He even later produced a music video mocking the incident. Although fellow music star Boy George complained 'You can get away with murder if you have the right PR machine'(*Daily Mirror*, 26 March 2005), Michael successfully used bigger-box thinking. By using the opportunity to confirm his homosexuality, he was able to redefine his situation and create a specific appeal for public sympathy for his apparent plight. He succeeded in minimizing the significance of his court case in the bigger context of gay rights.

Maximizing the significance

This is done by overstating or exaggerating the importance of one small paradigm, and ignoring, or understating, the significance of a larger host paradigm. You are essentially making your box larger than it merits. Political journalists Peter Oborne and Simon Walters (2004) describe the techniques used by Alastair Campbell, the former adviser to the British prime minister: 'A story might be fundamentally truthful and correct, but Campbell would seize on one minor detail or inaccuracy to create the impression that it was utterly false.' In paradigm terms a small box – part of a bigger paradigm – had its significance overstated.

Covering with something else

This involves using an unrelated paradigm to mask or cause a distraction from the original subject. You are using an unrelated big box to cover over your subject. On the day in 1997 when the Labour government in the UK was facing embarrassing stories relating to the then foreign secretary's extramarital affairs, a number of unrelated stories competed for media attention. The *Sunday Times* carried a front page sensational story alleging that the former governor of Hong Kong, Chris Patten, was facing possible prosecution under the Official Secrets Act. The allegation turned out to be groundless. The reason the story made the front page was that Downing Street had confirmed it. Other 'stories' to appear that day included reports of plans to stop the royal yacht *Britannia* from being scrapped. This story was also untrue. It appears that the spinning consisted of covering up one paradigm – the embarrassing story about the foreign secretary's private life – with other paradigms (Oborne and Walters, 2004).

This technique was also used by Yorkshire landscape artist Ashley Jackson when faced with a political question in a BBC local radio interview about wind farms on his beloved Pennine hillsides. Ashley, a keen conservationist, replied, 'Well I think wind power is a good thing. But I'm not too sure about having too many of them in one place. Why doesn't the government put them on the white cliffs of Dover instead?' He cleverly shifted the box away from his own personal position, covering it with another paradigm of the government's position. He also introduced to the debate an unrelated, but potent issue of north–south regional pride.

SANCTITY PARADIGMS

Communicators in a debate can sometimes come against the equivalent of a metaphorical brick wall: their opponent uses arguments such as 'health and safety', 'national security', 'the war against terrorism' or 'financial probity'. In these situations one side is using a 'sanctity paradigm', a platform of argument that it is difficult to establish a legitimate position against. No right-minded person would seemingly argue against health and safety, against security issues or for financial impropriety. The ground on which your opponent is arguing from is effectively sanctified.

A useful tactic when faced with a sanctity paradigm is to create an even higher paradigm level, using the 'intelligent paradigm'. Here what you are proposing is 'intelligent use of health and safety', 'intelligent defence of national security or war on terrorism', 'intelligent use of financial controls' and so on. In the example of the controversy in the UK surrounding the use of speed cameras by police forces to catch speeding motorists, opponents ultimately have difficulty arguing against the cameras when faced with the safety sanctity paradigm: the cameras are ostensibly there to save lives. This is difficult to argue directly against. What opponents should focus on is agreeing that speed cameras are a tool, able in certain instances to save lives, but arguing that they need to be employed intelligently. In paradigm terms they have established a new higher paradigm above the paradigm occupied by their opponents. (See Table 4.3.)

An alternative strategy in dealing with a sanctity paradigm is to use small-box thinking. If for example someone raised an objection because of 'health and safety', you could respond by asking, 'What aspect of health and safety is contravened?'

Table 4.3 *Dealing with sanctity paradigms: an example*

Self-interest	Road safety paradigm	Individual motorist's paradigm
	As an organization we need to undertake activity to ensure drivers drive slower to advance our beliefs and also demonstrate activity to justify our existence	As a driver I do not want to get an endorsement or pay a penalty fine
Common interest – 'sanctity paradigm'	Encouraging drivers to drive slower helps saves lives and reduces costs for the NHS. Therefore road safety cameras are a good thing.	It is hard for drivers to argue against this position as it appears they are arguing against a common and communal good. They need to move to a paradigm operating at a higher plane of interest.
Higher plane of interest	What is required is 'intelligent' use of road safety speed cameras. There needs to be a dialogue for people to have their say on the 'intelligent' application of safety cameras.	

By understanding that paradigms exist, you have a flexibility in recognizing and manipulating them. As a result the effective communicator can gain significant advantage over those stuck in 'same-box' thinking.

Task: putting it into practice

What examples of sanctity paradigms can you identify in your life? What sanctity paradigms can you create for your organization?

ALL IDEAS ARE IN 3D BOXES: INTRODUCING THE 'PARAMEME'

Paradigms provide a useful metaphor of a box to define the boundaries of a perception. Yet these boxes are essentially static snapshots of a reality at any one given time. Memes, in contrast, are inherently dynamic. They move beyond an existing paradigm to create further new messages, or reach out to new audiences beyond the original communication.

Communicators need a further tool to help them in managing the different dimensions of communication, combining the analysis of paradigms with how these boxes then engage with, and create their own dynamic, as a meme. The answer lies in the concept I have devised of a 'parameme' – the fusion between a paradigm and meme.

A parameme is essentially a three-dimensional paradigm containing descriptions of what the perceptions currently are, their history, coupled with their dynamic potential to be transmitted, replicated, and ultimately survive under their own volition. A parameme is essentially a paradigm with an engine, providing the tool for the communicator to assess the existing and potential value of a communication.

A parameme consists of three facets:

- a 'face' paradigm determining the current perception of the idea and its current context;
- a 'root' paradigm defining how deeply held is the perception;
- a 'connectivity' paradigm indicating the potential conductivity of a paradigm through its environment – its meme potential.

Face paradigm

The face paradigm consists of a snapshot of existing perceptions and underlying assumptions. This is coupled with assumptions about the context or marketplace within which the current idea operates (Figure 4.1). The face paradigm of a product, for example, will contain descriptions of what the product is, how it is used, when used and who by, where it is available, its value and how it is perceived in its particular marketplace.

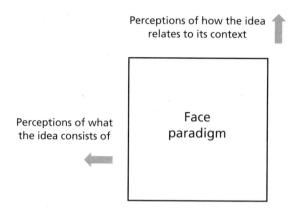

Figure 4.1 *Face paradigm*

Task: putting it into practice

Examine any campaign you have been involved with. What is the 'face paradigm' of your situation? What assumptions are being made about the benefits, uses, target markets and potential opposition to your planned activities? How does this 'face paradigm' compare with other campaigns?

Root paradigm

The 'root' paradigm defines the permanence of the face paradigm. How deeply entrenched is the idea in its context? The root paradigm is defined by time and history, in terms of permanence and how deeply held the paradigm is by the individual or marketplace (Figure 4.2).

Every time you use an idea you deepen its root paradigm. The longer you use a particular mental map, the harder it is for you to recognize its shortcomings. The more familiar a map becomes, the harder it is to accept the validity of anybody else's map of the same territory. The root paradigm of the example of a product would contain how long the product has been used for, its current and previous use, and frequency of use.

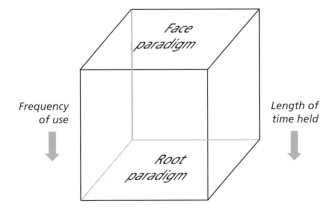

Figure 4.2   *Root paradigm*

Task: putting it into practice

Now you have examined your campaign's face paradigm, what is the extent of its root paradigm? How much awareness is there in its market-place about your campaign's product, service or issue? How easily can it be displaced by a competitor or apathy? How does this root paradigm compare with other campaigns?

Connectivity paradigm

The 'connectivity' paradigm (Figure 4.3) determines the extent and spread beyond the face paradigm and its responsiveness to change. The para-meme's pervasive dimension provides it with a dynamic element to grow beyond and out from its original position, and also be replaced by rival memes. The pervasive paradigm is determined by ease of outward connection/transmission/communication/replication, and ease of inward supplanting by a competing meme.

The connectivity paradigm for a product will feature its ease of use (and copyability), ease of getting it to new customers and markets, its potential for new applications or extensions of it. Every act and communication changes the parameme, either by extending the boundaries of the face paradigm, or by making the communication more entrenched and deepening its root paradigm, or extending its connectivity to extend its pervasiveness.

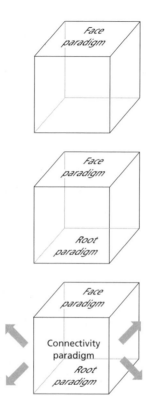

Figure 4.3 *Connectivity paradigm*

A parameme is a fusion of paradigms in three dimensions to provide a simplified cell structure – a box – to describe and analyse ideas, cultural and creative products, and communications. It is different from a meme because a parameme provides a tool for deconstructing memes. The meme is the sum of a parameme.

If you understand that every cultural and creative product is a uniquely shaped box, defined by the core variables of product assumption, context assumption, permanence and pervasiveness, coupled with the connectivity of these elements with their context, you have a relatively simple mechanism for reviewing and deconstructing your creative products and their potential for success.

On page 188 the contrasting paramemes of a computer nerd and Jesus Christ are compared.

> ### Task: putting it into practice
>
> What is the connectivity paradigm and what potential ways can you inter-
> act with your audiences and communications channels to extend your
> message? How does this 'connectivity paradigm' compare with other
> campaigns?

YOUR JOURNEY SO FAR

You have so far covered how communication starts from your inner
'brand' – how you think – and is propelled out by your interpersonal
skills. Your messages are conveyed by memes. You 'spin' paradigms to
frame how you would like your communications to be perceived. How do
you actually create effective messages? Read on in Chapters 5, 6 and 7.

PR FUTURES DEBATE

What is the 'public relations' meme? Has its spread been affected by its
degree of coherence and copyability?

Does the industry need to establish meme-friendly definitions for
itself?

Should PR practitioners be recognized as 'organization meme-
minders'?

PERSONAL CHECKLIST

● How meme-friendly are the messages you deliver?
● What paradigms are holding back your success as a communicator?
● How permanent and pervasive are the new paradigms you are trying
  to create in your communications?

PRELUDE TO CHAPTER 5

The message is the medium. You need to shape your messages to make
them meme and brand-friendly. You need to harness the power of icons in
your messages to make them distinctive and memorable. You communicate
and listen within the structure of a brand, values and beliefs. You need to
have clear positionings in your messages. Short is sweet.

5

The message is the medium – making your communications brand-friendly

One of the proudest moments in my working life happened when I was in a Leeds pub and overheard the barmaids' conversation. They were talking about a story one of them had heard on the news that morning – a story that, although they did not know this, I had created and issued. I had witnessed the power of communications in action: not just having my news broadcast, but seeing it subsequently relayed beyond from one person to another.

Marshall McLuhan in the 1960s wrote that 'the medium is the message' (McLuhan and Fiore, 2000). In the 21st century, in the age of indirect communications, with so many competing channels and the need to build credibility quickly, the dictum needs to be reversed: 'the message is the medium'.

Shaping and moulding your message is not just about ensuring you have the right content, or that it will achieve impact. You need to consider how your message can live on beyond, to have an after-life of its own, to reach out to new and different audiences.

The message can be the medium – if it is made 'sticky' and meme-friendly. To do this you need to examine the very core foundations and structure of language to identify what are the elements you need to manipulate and manage to make meme-friendly messages.

HOW THE STRUCTURE OF LANGUAGE INFLUENCES COMMUNICATION

Human beings' outstanding communications ability is not because of a specific biological advantage such as having bigger brains than other animals: whales and elephants have physically bigger brains, while mice brains are proportionally bigger than humans in relation to their body size. Although research is revealing greater understanding about the complexities of communications among other animals, no other species can match the sophistication of human language. What differentiates humans from other species is their ability to retain, store and transmit ideas and information. The key to this is found in two things: the processes involved in transmitting ideas, such as memes, and the structure of human language itself.

Humans excel in areas of language because of the make-up and disposition of their brains to capitalize on skills for language development, rather than their inherent size. In *The Symbolic Species* (1997), Terence Deacon argues that the process of evolution applied not only to human genetic development but also to language itself, evolving from a core structure into the sophisticated and complex vernacular of today. If you understand how language works you can then make it work more effectively in your communications.

Deacon identified that language is made up of three core elements:

● icons;
● symbols;
● indexical information.

Icons can be described as the ultimate image or point of reference in describing something. Iconic relationships are the most basic means of representation by being reduced to the point of no further reduction. It is where the referential buck stops, when nothing more is added – it is like the terminus of a perception.

If we were given the words 'New York City', each of us would conjure different images in our minds. Typically they could be scenes of skyscrapers, yellow cabs, food such as cheesecake or pastrami on rye sandwiches, graphic images like the Big Apple or the 'I♥NY' logo, or the news footage from 9/11. 'New York City' might be personified by people such as Mayor Giuliani, or the images could be more personal. As soon as the words 'New York City' are mentioned images immediately come to people's minds. Each single image that each of us conjures is an icon. This is not to state that it is a right answer, the universal icon for everyone to understand. It is what you individually create as a point of reference. It is what works for you.

An icon must provide further information in some way about the attributes of its object. An icon is the cornerstone of understanding and codifying different objects and realities. The word 'recognition' is actually 're-cognition' – to see again. The icon enables the item to be described and recognized again in a different context, as well as securing a deeper level of understanding and insight.

Icons work by what psychologists call 'primitive automacity', where you use only a single, highly representative piece of the total information to make a definitive statement about the whole. This is comically captured in a wonderful piece of repartee from the rock musician the late Frank Zappa. In the 1960s he was interviewed by vitriolic television chat show host Joe Pine, who was well known for having an artificial leg. The interview went like this:

> Joe Pine: 'I guess your long hair makes you a girl.'
> Frank Zappa: 'I guess your wooden leg makes you a table.'
> (Cialdini, 2001)

Symbols are created when you pair a sound, or a typed string of sounds and letters, with something else in the world. Symbolic media give you the power to share a virtual common mind. It is rather like different musicians who have never met before being able to perform a symphony together because they have a shared symbolic medium through musical notation.

Knitting together the use of icons and symbols are what is called 'indexical relationships'. These meet the need for continuity within a context, to explain a relationship between different items. They are used to describe comparative information such as hotter/colder, faster/slower, or more dangerous/safer.

Language arrived relatively late in humankind's communications development. This makes it less effective at conveying emotions than other core skills such as nonverbal communications. Individual communicators need to harness the power of nonverbal communications (as discussed in Chapter 3), and also structure their communications making full use of the potential of icons, symbols and indexical information. But how?

HOW THE STRUCTURE OF BRANDS SHOULD INFLUENCE COMMUNICATIONS

A 'brand' is the sum total of all the emotions, thoughts, images, history, possibilities and gossip that exists in a marketplace about a certain place, group, company, product, service, idea or even a person. A brand is not just a logo, or something just relevant to fast-moving consumer goods such as 'Coca-Cola' or 'Cadbury's' chocolate. It is the sum of all communications emanating from any given entity and the associations accorded to it by its context. Each of us is a living brand. Yes, you are a 'brand'.

In his or her professional role a public relations communicator could be defined as someone who is a one-person brand who instigates communications between a brand and its context.

Brands are made up of:

- icons;
- values;
- information.

(Note the similarity in the structure of a brand to the structure of language itself.) The outstanding individual communicator is a great manager of his or her own personal brand and the brands he or she is professionally seeking to communicate. Communicators achieve this through managing the different elements of icons, values and information.

A limitation of much communication activity is that it focuses solely on providing information, with any values only implicitly communicated, and no thought given to the use of icons in the message. Imagine a headless chicken trying to communicate. That is the reality of much current marketing communications. Effective communicators need to identify the different existing and potential elements of icons, values and information to ensure their communication is effective and sustainable.

ICONS

- Would the 'Millennium bug', the apocalyptical prediction of computer mayhem, have been so potent had it been called the '1998 bug'?
- What exactly did the former New York mayor, Rudolph Giuliani, do on 11 September 2001 to earn so much respect?
- Why is the former British prime minister Winston Churchill rated in surveys as one of the greatest Britons?

These are all examples of powerful icons. The Millennium bug neatly encapsulated a feeling in a society crossing a significant time threshold, where there was optimism about better future prospects combined with new fears and anxieties on entering a new millennium. The bug tapped into the negative undercurrent of the millennium. It was a catchy phrase, memorable, easy to say and visualize and tapped into core needs of security and order. The clear-cut, decisive actions of Mayor Giuliani during the events of 9/11 September and Winston Churchill in Britain's 'darkest hours' of 1940 offered hope and inspiration. They represented an innermost desire to achieve security, be resolute and provide self-belief and self-esteem at a difficult time. The men were great leaders at that particular moment in time, providing an emotional lightning rod, a rallying point. They acted as living icons, delivering the 'we-shall-survive-and-overcome meme', personifying people's hopes, allaying their fears and manifesting a desire for a better future. As a meme this message was able to circulate quickly in a period of great uncertainty.

The elements making up powerful icons are meme-friendly (they are coherent, copyable and live long enough to be passed on) and also appeal to the basic levels of need in Maslow's hierarchy (Maslow, 1954): the desire for security.

Icons are not just about major events and people. They can be evident in every area of communication, no matter how small in scale. The 'broken window' theory of crime, for example, where crime is regarded as a potentially contagious epidemic, starts from something small, such as the presence of a broken window in a community.

Marketing guru Seth Godin (2003) argues for a new 'P' to be added to the marketing lexicon of product, price, promotion and place: 'purple cow'. He justifies this from his experience on a holiday in France where his family got bored just looking at cows in the landscape. A 'purple cow', he felt, would really stand out, as representative of the challenge facing all organizations. Organizations need their own equivalent of a 'purple cow' to make them remarkable, by being original, distinctive, and memorable in their marketplace, getting them literally to stand out from the herd. Godin is in effect advocating an icon strategy, where communicators should tailor their offer around a 'purple cow' of a distinctive, memorable position to capture a share of people's minds and attention.

Have you ever wondered why most people only remember bits of songs? They remember the hook lines, the iconic high points in the song's landscape, but are often fuzzy about the words in-between. Even individual words have their own iconic structure. Read the sentence below:

Aoccdrnig to rscheearch by the Chratreed Isntite of Pbulic Rletaoins, it deosn't mttaer in what oredr the ltteers in a wrod are. The olny iprmoetnt tihng is taht the frist and lsat ltteer are in the rghit pclae. The rset can be a toatl mses and you can sitll raed it. Tihs is bcuseae the huamn mnid deos not raed ervey lteter by istlef, but the wrod as a wlohe.

The data you receive and communicate, like words themselves, is not a sequential composite, but is rather made up of initially accepting an icon within the message to give you a cue to its whole meaning. The icon acts as a heuristic device, a rule of thumb, to enable you to make sense of something bigger. Icons have the power to create the impression of being the totality of something. If you want your message to achieve impact and be sustainable, fundamentally you need to check that it contains a memorable icon. The fashion company French Connection profitably capitalized on this process with its brand 'Fcuk'.

MANAGING ICONS

Icon management falls into three distinct situations.

Icon abundance

Here there are many highly visible or memorable icons. Good examples are major international cities such as New York City and London, and organizations such as Manchester United Football Club (with its red shirts, individual legendary players, the tragedy of the Munich air crash, and more recently its 'Theatre of Dreams' branding for the Old Trafford stadium). The strategy here is to prioritize, or use selectively specific icons for certain situations, or even rotate the primacy of individual icons.

Icon singularity

Here the paradigm is known just for one key thing. The city of Nottingham in the UK for example went into a form of 'Robin Hood denial' in the 1990s, when it sought to achieve wider recognition for other things beyond the legend of Robin Hood and his 'merrie men' in Sherwood Forest. Potential strategies for icon singularity include investing further in the core icon to achieve optimum results, or investing in specific possibly small niche icons to complement and get leverage from the core icon.

Icon absence

Here there is no icon, or existing icons have a limited value, profile or exposure. The initial job in these situations is to identify what under-promoted icons or seeds of potential icons exist, and develop strategies to transform their status. Niche strategies can be highly cost-effective. The Lancashire seaside resort of Morecombe in the UK for example switched the money it had previously spent on its Christmas lights to hosting one of the world's biggest punk music festivals.

Note that an icon must tell you more about something. Communicators need to be wary of 'big idea' strategies. The town of Soap Lake, Washington State, USA, which plans to create a new landmark for itself by installing the world's largest lava lamp, will find its communications value and sustainability limited unless the town already has significant lava lamp credentials or connections, such as being the place where it was invented, or invests further in sustaining the message about its icon. (Visit www.worldslargestdoc.com for other American examples of places with vacuous claims to fame, from the world's largest 'talking cow' to largest crow statue.)

A tactic when there are no readily available potential icons to use in your message, or you are trying to relate to someone who does not know you, is to use a metaphor. For example, at a job interview I once described myself using the qualities of two well-known British footballers of the 1980s: 'I work hard like Bryan Robson, but have the creative flair of Glenn Hoddle.' (I didn't get the job!)

ICON STRATEGY MAPS

A simple tool for developing an icon strategy is an icon strategy map. This tool was used in a project for the West Yorkshire based Wakefield Development Agency. In addressing the challenge of how the district should promote itself, research revealed two key problems. First, the area had low unprompted awareness (that is, positive responses to the question, 'Do you know where Wakefield is?'). Contingent with this fact, the district did not have any iconic awareness: people not only did not know where it was, they also did not know what it should be known for. The advice given to the development agency was that rather than a costly awareness programme, it should invest initially in an icon strategy. The strategy consists of identifying existing and potential icons, and classifying them according to their potential level of interest. The agency could decide which existing icons to invest in further and promote, while also examining potential icons for both their individual potential and any wider synergy with other icons. Table 5.1 shows that Wakefield actually has plenty to boast about.

The icon strategy map analysis revealed that the Wakefield district had potentially strong icons in the Yorkshire Sculpture Park, one of the world's leading outdoor art venues, along with a host of other historic

Table 5.1 *An icon league table for the Wakefield district*

Level	Description	Type	Suggestions
1	World quality venue/ facility/theme/identity/ claim to fame	If you have visitors from overseas you would consider taking them to/ showing them this to highlight a key point of interest	Yorkshire Sculpture Park Sculpture greats – Henry Moore, Barbara Hepworth World's first nature reserve – Walton Hall/Charles Waterton Trail* Birthplace of John Harrison* (solved the problem of how to find longitude at sea) World's first public railway* Robin Hood birthplace* Centre of Universe Centre* 'Mulberry bush' and 'Grand Old Duke of York' nursery rhymes originated here*
2	National quality venue/ facility/theme/identity Already established Distinct national positioning Competing with other national attractions Difficult for a competitor to copy Attracts visitors nationally	If you have visitors from outside the region you would consider taking them to/showing them this to highlight a key point of interest	National Mining Museum Nostell Priory Pontefract Castle Sandal Castle Wakefield Prison Heath Village Trail* Rhubarb Festival Liquorice Festival* Legend of Highwayman William Nevison* English Civil War Trail* Richard III tour* Town/country balance message* Heart of Yorkshire message*

Table 5.1 *An icon league table for the Wakefield district (continued)*

Level	Description	Type	Suggestions
3	Regional quality venue/ facility Regional positioning Already offered to some degree by a competitor Attracts visitors regionally	If you have visitors from within the region you would consider taking them to/showing them this to highlight a key point of interest	Fairburn Ings country park Bretton Country Park Wakefield Cathedral District town centres George Gissing museum Freeport Burberry factory shop Theatre Royal and Opera House, Wakefield Castleford Roman archaeology*
4	District-wide quality venue/facility District positioning Attracts visitors from across the district and wider area	You would go across the district to visit	Wakefield Museum Wakefield Art Gallery New Millerdam Country Park Pugneys Water Park Hemsworth Water Park Thornes Park Arts Centre Lightwaves Leisure Centre Woolley Edge scenic views

*Indicates an idea or project where further development work is required.

claims not marked in any formal way. One benefit of unearthing potential opportunities is that potential icons can lead to serendipity-like linkages. It subsequently emerged that there are plans to redevelop the city's mainline railway station, which would seem an appropriate opportunity to incorporate some marking of the district's claim to have the world's first public railway.

Potential icons may only exist at an embryonic stage, but can offer potential for outrageous positioning. Plans by the West Yorkshire Astronomy

Group to create the world's first public observatory for disabled people in the district inspired the author to suggest a new potential branding of the new observatory as the 'Centre of the Universe Centre', on the basis that somewhere has got to be the centre of the universe, so why not Wakefield in the UK?

Task: putting it into practice

What are your icons? Now you know about icons and how they act as fundamental defining points to achieve recognition, what are your personal icons that communicate you to the outside world?

- What is it in the way you appear to the outside world others remember you by?
- What are the key talents and skills you are known for?
- What are your achievements others note?
- What are you remembered for?
- What does your icon strategy map look like?

NAMES

The most important word in the world is your name. Names are one of the most commonly used icons. Giving something a name clearly identifies it and labels the new from the old. When something is named it becomes 'thinkable'. Names are not just relevant for the totality of the object, but can be used to mark out smaller elements. For one building product company making temporary fencing for the construction industry, I created the brand name 'smartweld' to describe the new-style welding joint featured in the fence. I knew it was successful when two years later I saw a small ad in an Irish newspaper offering second-hand fencing and boasting that it featured 'smartweld joints'. Someone completely independent of the manufacturer was spreading the brand name.

Care needs to be taken that you do not create an overload of brand names and identities, which can only lead to confusion or cynicism over how 'new' the initiative actually is. A brand review exercise I undertook with a further education college was a particular eye-opener on the problem of brand profusion, particularly in the public sector. When they were asked how many brands they had to directly and indirectly manage, instead of an expected three or four the group identified over 20 initiatives. The college had faced a government initiative overload. The strategy here is to undertake a brand culling – to reduce the number of brands to a manageable size – or establish a brand hierarchy, creating clear relationships between the multifarious brands.

Task: putting it into practice

When it comes to the brands and names you use, what is your job title? Does it accurately reflect who you are and what you do?

Communicators do have a responsibility to be neologists, to create new names to add to the general vocabulary to meet the needs of a rapidly expanding world. By creating a name you potentially create a clear-cut label to make the element you are describing distinctive and memorable.

Perhaps the most outrageous – and earliest – example of creating a name to establish a memorable marketing message was that of Erik the Red, the founder and creator of the name 'greenland' which became a colony for Norse settlers. As naturalist Jared Diamond (2005) observed on his first visit to the country, 'My initial impression of Greenland [from the air] was its name was a cruel misnomer, because I only saw a three coloured-landscape: white, black and blue, with white overwhelmingly predominant . . .'. Maybe Erik the Red needed a catchy, inspiring meme to attract potential migrants to a harsh, tough land and hence inspired the name 'Greenland'.

Another example of the potency of names is the campaign by fundamentalists in the United States for creationism to be taught in schools. Seeking to overcome a Supreme Court ruling that 'creationism' was a religious belief, they started using new, more scientific-sounding terms and phraseology such as 'abrupt appearance theory' and 'intelligent design theory' to disguise the fact that their only textbook was the Old Testament (Wheen, 2004).

Task: putting it into practice

What names can you create for tasks which may be new or specific to a situation? Can you create new brand names or words to describe specific activities in your next communication?

VALUES AND INFORMATION

A brand is like an egg. Its overall shape and appearance are part of its iconic qualities – you see the image of the egg and you think this is an 'egg'. Its shell is a metaphor for containing the hardcore information about it, and similarly its yolk represents its values, containing subliminal qualities of heritage, inner strength, reassurance and essence.

Most marketing communications operate solely on the level of managing information. Although facts and figures, like the eggshell, provide the hard-core and evident substance of a brand, they are not the sum of the brand. By identifying existing values on a personal or organizational level, you can gain leverage and make your communications more sustainable.

VALUES AUDIT

Every communication contains values. For the most part they are imparted implicitly. If you examine a selection of different communications and note every value-laden statement, it is possible to identify the values implicit in the communication. A number of techniques can be used to map out the values, for example laddering or cobweb analysis.

An example of a company's values hierarchy: GREEN brand communications

These are the values of Wakefield-based public relations company GREEN brand communications, where I am a partner.

By using our expert skills, time, and networks GREEN is:

1. Paranoid – about achieving the best results for its clients
2. Straight – telling things honestly, taking responsibility, and building genuine, committed relationships
3. Intelligent – in its thinking, using creativity to add value
4. Resourceful – making best use of resources and opportunities.
5. Committed to a better world – seeking to make the lives of our clients, colleagues and community better in some way.

An example of an individual's values hierarchy – the author's

An interesting juxtaposition is provided by my personal values. Note how there are some similarities, but they are not the same as the values of the organization where I play a key role.

1. *I hate waste* – whether it is wasting resources, creative ideas or new opportunities. I am passionate about people realizing their potential because they could waste the opportunity before them. I hate it when a great idea gets knocked back because it represents a wasted opportunity.
2. *I don't want to conform* – I am curious about new things and challenging orthodoxy. People saying it can't be done provides me with the biggest motivator to prove them wrong. I try to inject fun into the most unlikely of occasions, believing that humour is the most powerful anarchic tool.
3. *Compassion* – I am no saint but if in a position to help someone, I will.
4. *Responsibility* – I am personally accountable whether it is about my own life, or my role in my community. I cannot just sit back. It is up to me to get things sorted.
5. *Laziness* – I am incredibly lazy. Most people think I am a workaholic; it is just a façade. If there is a short cut I will take it. If I do a lot of work it is because I am incompetent in my laziness. (I am not going to say any more about this – I cannot be bothered!)

Your own values

You can establish a hierarchy of these values by doing the 'rule number one' test. Which values take precedence over the others? For example, even when I am in a desperate hurry I cannot leave the house without making sure the lights are switched off – rule number one of my hating waste kicks in and determines my behaviour.

When establishing your values and values hierarchy you should ideally have no more than five individual value statements. People cannot remember more than five things. Any more than five values and you will have difficulty remembering them, making them less copyable as a meme, and undermining their sustainability.

Much of current public relations communications practice focuses solely on information: facts, features, details about a subject. More crucial to meme-friendly information is the use of icons to assist coherence and memorability, along with values to build a commonality to enable you to connect with other people. The information content in your message should play a supporting role in your message, and is not the sum of the message.

Once you have established your potential icons, values and information you need to structure your message by establishing a positioning and creating a series of brand platforms.

Task: putting it into practice

What are your values?

- What is important to you? (In what ways is it important, and what need does it fulfil?)
- What is your values hierarchy?
- What are the values of your communication targets?
- How are their values different from yours?
- What common values do you have?
- How can you adapt your values and the values of your target audience to build a bridge between you?

POSITIONING

The typical person going on a diet is more professional than most marketing communications programmes. The first thing dieters do is weigh themselves and then set a target weight loss to achieve. At the very least, even if they are unsuccessful in their goal, they put in place a framework to manage the challenge. The cornerstone of a framework for personal communications – the equivalent of weighing yourself during a diet – is the use of 'positioning' and creating a 'positioning statement.'

The positioning statement should explain four things:

- What you do – your products or services.
- Who you do it for – your prime customers.
- What makes you unique – your unique selling proposition (usp).
- How you substantiate your uniqueness – how you can justify and lay claim to make a 'unique' offer.

The basic approach to positioning is not to create something new and different, but to manipulate what is already there in the mind of your target audience. The positioning should seek to retie the connections that already exist. In an age of communication clutter and information overload, it is better to work on the premise that little of your message will get through. The positioning is designed to overcome the challenge of people coping with complexity by simplifying everything.

The first stage in seeking a solution to your positioning is to look not within yourself but rather in your prospects' minds, and concentrate on their existing perceptions. What is their existing awareness, perception and empathy with you?

The next stage is to identify what particular messages you have. The easiest way for you to gain impact is to secure primacy into someone's mind, to be first in your field. By getting first you effectively imprint your stake to owning a share of mind in your target audience. The importance of primacy is as a result of 'imprinting', a term biologists use to describe the first encounter between a newborn baby and its natural mother. The importance of primacy cannot be overstated. Think how you remember the first, but never the second in a list. What is the name of the second person to have run the four-minute mile? What is the name of the world's second-highest mountain?

If you are genuinely a clear-cut first in what you are doing, you just need to articulate your position clearly. For most communicators, however, the challenge is how is it possible to be 'first' in a well-established market. The answer is through using smaller-box thinking and identifying specific niches, angles or opportunities to provide the foundation for your positioning. Alternatively, you can use bigger-box thinking and look for a more global issue to which to relate your positioning.

Successful communications create a position in the prospect's mind, and also take into account your own strength and weaknesses, and those of competing messages. Establishing these details provides the foundations to one side of the bridgehead you are creating in your communications between you and your target audience.

The challenge in creating an effective positioning is to establish a unique position with an appeal that is not too narrow. A good guiding rule as advocated by Luke Sullivan in his *Hey, Whipple Squeeze This!* (2003) is to: 'Plant your flag on the highest mountain you can.'

The first rule of positioning is that in order to win the battle for the mind you cannot compete head-on against a company that has a strong established position. The existing market leader owns the high ground, the number one position. What counts most is the receptivity of both parties to the message: the sender and the receiver must both be receptive to the message.

A positioning is shaped by its context, a fact which one opportunistic politician recognized: Luther D Knox, a candidate in the Louisiana gubernational primary, changed his name by deed poll to 'None of the Above'. A federal judge ruled against his new name being on the ballot, claiming it was deceptive!

Positioning is not about securing what you believe is good about you: it is about what is credible about you. As the great creative writer Howard Gossage said, 'If you got a lemon, make lemonade.' Even if your asset is not universally popular it might still present niche opportunities. My own favourite positioning for a place is the Canadian town I came across when hitch-hiking across North America in 1978. On the town perimeter a large hoarding proudly boasted the town's name and claim to fame: 'Sudbury – famous for its pollution'!

Robin Wight of brand agency wrcs emphasizes the importance of taking into account people's preconceptions when shaping your message or meme:

> When producing a meme you not only need to identify what will make a spreadable message. You also need to understand how the brain works and appreciate it will only allow certain things in. The brain is very lazy and will programme itself to accept only things it perceives to meet a need. Our agency [wcrs] has devised a concept of 'differentiated continuity' where we are able to spread a message that has to be compatible with memes already present in the brain.

You need to ensure you don't just create a meme without thinking through the wider brand message. The beer brand Budweiser produced a memorable international campaign using 'wassup' as a catchphrase. It failed in the longer term as it failed to create any wider association with the brand. You may know the slogan but where does it take you? All people were left with was a memorable phrase which perpetuated beyond the life of the accompanying campaign and probably undermines by getting in the way of any subsequent brand activity.

Task: putting it into practice

Write a positioning statement for yourself or your organization. Write a new positioning about you or your organization set in the future. How is it different from the present?

BRAND PLATFORMS

The challenge in communicating a brand is that you potentially have 1,001 different messages to say about your brand. How can you deliver this scale of messages in a credible, effective way? The answer is to identify a series of brand platforms. These platforms provide in effect a series of subheadings to classify the many different messages inherent in the brand. The brand platform consists of key issues, or themes, which provide a coherent grouping for a range of different messages.

Ideally there should be no more than around five different brand platforms. This is to again ensure sustainability of the message, so that brand messengers can remember most of the core messages. For example, the brand platforms of this book could be:

- maximizing your skills as a public relations communicator by harnessing your personal skills and the brilliant potential of all people to communicate and transform their world;
- messages, memes and paramemes – making them established tools in marketing communications thinking and harnessing the power of icons and values to create meme-friendly messages;
- extending the boundaries of public relations practice to include networking, viral, word-of-mouth and word-of-click communications;
- the concept of 'personal brandcasting' (see Chapter 11) – how your dreams, memes and teams can create tidal waves of communications through more sophisticated use of your networks.

Task: putting it into practice

What are the brand platforms in your communications? Create five brand platforms in your next campaign.

THE MEME-FRIENDLY MESSAGE

To make your messages meme-friendly they need to have a memorable hook. Icons act as these hooks. They must also be coherent and copyable. A positioning provides a completeness about your description, and enables you to provide a form and shape to your message to enhance its copyability.

Ready coherence

A fundamental responsibility in communications is to translate your data or ideas, and package them to make them understandable for target markets but also to facilitate their wider transmission. The ancient Greek goddess of memory is Mnemosyne. Not many people seem to remember her; her cause is not helped by her having a difficult name to pronounce or memorize. Your message needs to be relatively simple to make it coherent and copyable.

Any idea what 'deoxyribonucleic acid' is? It is in fact one of our society's most significant scientific discoveries. Widespread reference and awareness was made easier by adopting the acronym DNA. Adolf Hitler originally called his book *My 4½ year struggle against lies, stupidity and cowardice*, until the publisher suggested the snappier title of *Mein Kampf* (My struggle). The Lord's Prayer is just 56 words long, the Ten Commandments 297 words, the Declaration of Independence of the United States some 300 words. (A typical government bill is over 30,000 words long!)

President John F Kennedy in creating a memorable meme for the US space programme in the 1960s could have stated the goal of the programme as 'to make some key improvements in order to establish the US as a leader in space exploration', which does not really excite the imagination. At the time the most optimistic scientific assessment of the moon mission's chances for success was 50/50 and most experts were more pessimistic. Despite this Congress immediately agreed to invest US $549 million straight away and billions more in the following five years. Kennedy was successful because of the 'stickiness factor' in his vision – 'that this nation should commit itself to achieving the goal, before this decade is out, of landing a man on the moon and returning him safely to earth'. It made the message inspiring, exciting and it 'stuck'.

The elevator speech – the briefest description of your sales pitch to fit in the time it would take to ride several floors in an elevator – is the epitome of communications brevity. In the fast-moving world of Hollywood the outstanding elevator speech is the difference between success and failure. Hollywood is full of people selling the next blockbuster idea with pitches such as: 'It's a bit like *The Matrix* meets *Mission: Impossible.*' Hollywood folklore records how Steven Spielberg sold the concept for *E.T.* as 'lost alien befriends lonely boy to get home', while the makers of *Top Gun* simply showed a mocked-up photograph of Tom Cruise on an aircraft carrier, saying 'We want to make a film of this,' to persuade backers.

Even place names should be short and snappy. Ries and Trout in their marketing classic *Positioning* (2001) demonstrate a two-syllable rule for place names: Los Angeles at four syllables long is evidently far too strenuous for local tongues, and the two-syllable acronym 'LA' is used. Interesting San Francisco is not 'SF' because the alternative 'Frisco' is two-syllable, and New Jersey is not called 'NJ' because again 'Jer-sey' obliges in just two syllables. It appears when people have a choice between a word or initials of the same phonetic length, they use words, not acronyms. Research among company names reveals that names are more memorable than acronyms.

The tragedy of 9/11 created some outstanding brand concepts. The people of the United States were faced with the wasted site of the former World Trade Center. The brand 'Ground Zero' provides a valuable com-munication tool, which on one level described the reality of the site as a flattened waste, and yet on another level captures the aspiration and hope for the site as the foundations of a new beginning.

OUTSTANDING COMMUNICATORS SHAPE THEIR MESSAGE

By understanding that their message can be shaped by managing the icons and values within it, and not just focusing on its information content, outstanding communicators can boost the likelihood of their message getting through to its target, but also being remembered.

PR FUTURES DEBATE

Should public relations managers be in charge of managing their organization's icons and values? Why does the subject of values currently reside, if anywhere in organizations, in human resources departments? As values are a dimension to communications, should they be under the control of the public relations professional?

Do we need a word for our responsibility to create new words in marketing communications?

PERSONAL CHECKLIST

- What are your icons?
- What is it in the way you appear to the outside world that others remember you by?
- What are the key talents and skills you are known for?
- What are your achievements that others note?
- What are you remembered for?
- What does your icon strategy map look like?
- What are your values?
- What is your values hierarchy?
- What are the values of your communication targets?
- How are their values different from yours?
- What common values do you have?
- What is your positioning?
- What are your brand platforms?
- Are messages about you readily coherent?

PRELUDE TO CHAPTER 6

You can shape your message to be potentially meme-friendly, yet will it provoke change? The final element in a message is its call to action, to make things happen. Your message needs to be trigger-friendly, so that it can make the connection between your new communication and getting your target to act.

You can achieve this by building commonality with your target audience, exploiting benefits, using key messages, communicating with flair and flourish, and tailoring your communication as much as possible to the target.

If a picture can paint a thousand words, a metaphor can deliver a million bayonets.

6

Triggering your message to achieve change

Your message can be shaped to be potentially memorable and meme-friendly, yet will it provoke change? The final element in a message is its call to action, to make things happen. Your message needs to be trigger-friendly, so that it can make the connection between your meme and making your targets act, or change their behaviour.

David Ogilvy (2004) pays tribute to the ability to create change through their communications that was the hallmark of the outstanding Classical orator: 'When Aeschines spoke they said, "How well he speaks." But when Demosthenes spoke, they said, "Let us march against Philip." I'm for Demosthenes.' In a more contemporary setting, left-wing comedian Mark Steel (2002) similarly recalls how during the UK miners' strike of 1984, 'Miners could make great speeches about why you should support them; miners' wives could demand you supported them, and if you already supported them, that you should support them more.'

Whether you are a Greek orator, or a striking miner's wife, key requirements to achieving change in your communications are:

- reducing dissonance;
- meeting a need;
- starting from the present;
- selling benefits;
- using influencing facts to persuade;
- delivering your message with brio;
- making your message bespoke.

DISSONANCE

Your life is spent reducing 'dissonance'. Dissonance is the feeling you get when you have just done something and need to reassure yourself you made the right decision. Dissonance is the unease you experience when someone tells you something is black but you see it as plainly white, and are being asked to change your view. Holding two simultaneous different beliefs in your mind can cause you discomfort, or the feeling that something is somehow not right. The feeling motivates you to reduce this dissonance and achieve consonance, a feeling of balance in your mind that things are all right after all.

The magnitude of dissonance depends on the:

- importance of the decision;
- relative importance of the different elements;
- proportions in which different elements are dissonant;
- perceived overlap between two objects (it is easier to make a consumer choice between say two different stereo systems rather than choose between buying a stereo or a computer).

You can reduce dissonance and achieve consonance by:

- changing one of the elements;
- giving reasons to justify the choice, no matter how 'illogical';
- altering the importance of the different elements;
- making the option appear compatible with your existing values;
- focusing on a small detail, using smaller-box thinking, to establish common agreement with the target;
- establishing a far bigger context, using bigger-box thinking, to create a position of 'In the grand scheme of things such differences are not important after all';
- putting the message in the positive: people dislike losses and feel it is more painful to give up than to gain.

Take the example of football fanatics who support their team with a deeply held passion and sense of pride. If you ask them to support another club you will face extreme resistance. Yet if you were to ask, 'What do you think of such and such a player?' you could achieve consonance by getting agreement on just one minor part of the other team's paradigm. Alternatively, if the opposing team was in an international tournament, playing a club from an unfavoured nation, rival fans might support it in that particular match as it is representing their country. They can achieve consonance by combining small-box thinking – that they are only supporting the opposition for a limited time-frame of just one match – and bigger-box consonance, that the other team is the representative of their national interest. Your communication will fail if it seeks to persuade someone head-on to change teams, because the dissonance would be too great and uncomfortable.

An example of how each of us manipulate our perspective of experiences to justify our existing situation, and thereby reduce dissonance, is given by Mihaly Csikszentmihalyi in his study (1997) of creative people where he asked them about their childhoods. One case provided an interesting example of changing perspectives:

> An extremely successful young artist in 1963 described his childhood as perfectly normal, even idyllic. Ten years later he was having trouble professionally .... Now he began to mention events in his childhood that were definitely less rosy .... Ten years later still, the artistic career of this no longer young man was pretty much washed up .... Now his description of his childhood included alcoholic fathers and uncles, physical abuse and emotional tyranny. No wonder the child had failed as an adult. Which version of his early years was closer to the truth? Did his therapy help him see more clearly a past he had repressed? Or did the helpful therapist provide him with a script that explained, and excused, why he had failed?

If an idea, or meme, seems well-founded to most people exposed to it, non-hosts will adopt and retain it because it does not create dissonance. In communications it is essential to analyse the potential dissonance your communication might create. Like the artist described by Csikszent-mihalyi, your audience might be using coping strategies of denial or imposing false memory to make their current worldview more tolerable. It is possible, through flexibly adapting the paradigms of the message, using either or both of smaller and bigger-box thinking, to change perceptions or recognize the different perceptions adopted by your target audience.

YOU NEED A NEED TO COMMUNICATE

Why do we perceive some things as more important than others? Abraham Maslow (1954) developed the concept of a hierarchy of needs. Our needs span from basic wants of food, shelter, sex and feeling safe through to fulfilling our emotional and artistic desires. If our lower needs are not satisfied we concentrate exclusively on satisfying them. When these lower needs are filled to an acceptable level, we can begin to put our energies into fulfilling our higher needs. While you can sate your basic needs you might never have enough love or respect.

When communicating you should take into account the context of the audience's prime needs: if people currently fear for their survival they certainly will not be receptive to listening to any comparatively trivial piece of information. You can also gain leverage in your communication by linking your messages to the relevant needs of your audience.

'Hurt and rescue' is a common ploy manipulating dissonance used by salespeople. They firstly heighten a sense of fear – 'Do you mean your loved ones are not protected because you are not insured?' – then provide a solution to a need which you previously were not aware of, or had not thought important. Michael Regester is a leading expert in crisis management. When shaping a message in a crisis he identifies the needs and fears among different stakeholders to shape his messages and tactics during a crisis situation: 'You have to identify what are the real emotional triggers and any specific needs which require your response and also how you will stop any perceived risks or how you intend to make things better.'

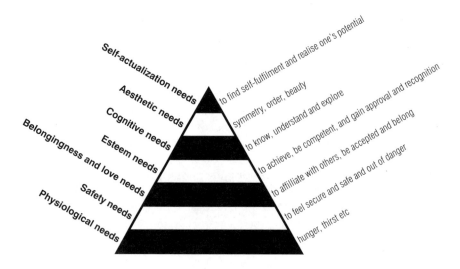

Figure 6.1 *Pyramid of needs*

Task: putting it into practice

Review any recent campaigns. How did you relate to needs in your messages? Reflect on any recent negotiation or client relationship challenges. What are the different needs of the parties involved? Review the messages contained within a newspaper or broadcast. What needs are contained in their messages?

THE MIXTURE OF MOTIVATIONS

What makes people tick in terms of what they strive for in their daily lives? If you can identify people's key motivators you can make your message more appealing. Personal development guru Anthony Robbins (2001) identified five key motivators for people:

- Certainty, where people fundamentally want to feel comfortable and avoid pain. Therefore any message should minimize any perceptions of risk. This need for certainty creates an inherent conservatism and serves as a default mode in people's thinking. Whenever faced with change people's initial tendency will be to resist and maintain a status quo – the certainty of misery is better than the misery of uncertainty. Human behaviour is also often driven by the desire to conform to authority.
- A need for uncertainty, seeking surprise and variety in their lives. This may seem paradoxical but it is couched in the context of people not believing they will compromise their fundamental survival for the sake of variety. Although white-water rafting, for example, is dangerous, people do it expecting to survive the experience. There is what can be called a 'bungee jump syndrome' of change, or danger being confronted when there is the reassurance of some form of safety rope or net.
- Significance, where people want to feel important and unique. The self-esteem of the target needs to be considered in any communication. If people feel patronized they will resist your message.
- Love and emotional connection, an ultimate level of actualization.
- Growth, the need to nurture new within the old, recognizing a natural momentum that if you stop growing you start dying.

If you tailor your communication to meet the motivational needs of an audience it will enhance your potential success.

Task: putting it into practice

What motivations are at work when you are managing a conflict situation or a relationship? Review a recent communication. How are the motivations of others different to yours?

BUILD A BRIDGE TO THE FUTURE – FROM THE PRESENT

The fundamental starting point for communicating is not deciding what you want to say. Rather it is identifying what people want to hear. Outstanding communicators work back from where their prospects are residing, in communications terms. You start from the target – their existing mental map – and work back to where your message is. You then adapt what you would like to say to fit in with your target's mental map. By adopting this process you can enable your targets to embark on a journey, moving from their existing position to a new point of view.

Regan Cooper, a specialist in community relations, points out how this understanding of other people's needs is crucial in sponsorship activity: 'Far too many community groups and charities approach organizations for money or support but fail to check the fundamental fact of what it is they can actually offer their sponsor, from the perspective of the sponsor.' It cannot be overstated how important listening skills are to the effective communicator. Respecting that other people have something to offer is the first step in building effective communications with them.

Dale Carnegie, in his seminal work on persuasion, *How to Win Friends and Influence People* (1953), recognized that people are not creatures of logic but of emotion. The only way to get anyone to do anything is to make the other person want to do it. You influence other people by talking about what they want and showing them how to get it.

Consider the major branding issues faced on one of the most divisive of issues – abortion. The campaigners against abortion adopt a position of 'pro life', making it hard for someone to say, 'Well actually, I am not pro life.' Those taking a contrary position use the branding 'pro choice', where they are adopting a stance behind a woman's right to choose. This moves the issue away from life and death to respecting and allowing adults to make choices about their lives. The rival groups on the abortion issue have created platforms to establish as much commonality with as many different people as possible.

SELL BENEFITS, LEGITIMACY AND DRAMATIC DIFFERENCE

Most practitioners know how messages should contain benefits – what will it do for me? – rather than just describe features. Nobody buys washing powder: people buy the ability to make clothes clean. Yet you can skilfully make your benefits proposition work even harder by clarifying key benefits and substantiating their validity. This not only highlights the inherent quality of the benefits but also boosts their credibility and believability.

A benefits proposition in any message should contain:

- overt benefits to the target;
- real reasons to believe;
- dramatic differences you offer;
- links to a key motivator where possible.

Overt benefits

People listen to only one radio station, WIIFM – what's in it for me – as Doug Hall emphasizes in his *Jump Start Your Business Brain* (2002). Spelling out the overt benefits in your message assists the replication and travel quality of your communication. A process for turning features into benefits consists of deconstructing the attributes of the situation. List the obvious and less obvious points of difference between your and competing messages. Work to transform each feature into a benefit by using these checklist questions:

- Why should you care about a feature?
- Why is it important?
- Why does the competition not offer this element?
- What first inspired your brand to start in the first place?
- What injustice is your brand seeking to address?
- What are you most proud about in relation to what your organization does for its customers?
- What do your most loyal customers boast about?
- What are you the best/first/only brand to offer?
- What negatives can be transformed into positives?
- What specific targets or niches can you focus on?

- How can you visualize your benefits?
- What do your benefits feel like?
- What do your benefits sound like?
- What would your benefits smell like?

A technique to develop your sagacity for benefits spotting that is recommended by Doug Hall is to review your recent credit card statement and examine the benefit you gained from each purchase. Doing this enhances your sensitivity to identifying benefits in your communications.

In making benefits claims in your messages, beware of solving a problem that is not really a problem. A company once launched a heating radiator made from aluminium. Its key benefit was its lightness. The only person who marginally gained from this benefit was the installer, not the specifier or customer, the crucial decision makers for the purchase. Some benefits might not be appropriate for certain circumstances. Low price is a benefit in the battle between supermarkets but will not be appropriate for luxury items.

You also need to ensure your message is addressing what marketing expert John Timperley calls a 'considered need' rather than an 'unconsidered need'. If someone talks about problems, difficulties or dissatisfactions, by beginning a sentence with: 'I am not happy with ...' he or she is expressing an unconsidered need, which does not automatically mean that he or she wants it immediately solved. In contrast, if he or she says, 'My objective is ...' or 'What I am asking for ...' then he or she is talking about what he or she expressly wants, and potentially requires your help.

Real reason to believe

In order for a message to be perceived as credible it must have a 'legitimizer'. This substantiates and provides credibility for the overt benefit claims. Legitimizers in a message are ideally hard factual details, such as previous track record, size and scale of the offer, expertise, blue-chip customers or individual connections.

Legitimizing your message goes beyond just the content of the message. The status of the person or organization delivering the message is significant: a message from a CEO will be perceived as more important than one from a lowly executive. How the message is presented is also relevant: a conference-style delivery with full-gloss brochures could be taken more credibly than something written on the back of a napkin.

Legitimacy is crucial to ensuring wider delivery of your message. By using legitimizers in your benefits proposition, you are reducing potential dissonance. You are helping to minimize potential anxieties which could undermine your targets' receptivity to your message. It can also pay to target your message to smaller specific niches rather than wide-ranging audiences. If you focus on a specific target market you immediately enhance your perception as an expert – and can gain further leverage from this expert position. Your pedigree can provide the confidence to potential customers, if you detail the heritage behind yourself, your product or service.

Visibility can also provide a legitimizing influence. The Nazi propaganda minister Joseph Goebbels recognized that repetition of information increases its perceived validity, rather as Lewis Carroll observed in 'The hunting of the Snark': 'What I tell you three times is true.' Seeing is believing; if something is widely manifest and visible it provides perceived confirmatory evidence. Everyone is talking about it, it creates an impression of evident truth. This phenomenon led the novelist Norman Mailer to coin the term 'factoid' – a fact only substantiated by its presence in the media.

You can use your personal authority or link the source of your message to another body recognized as significant to endorse the validity of your meme and provide it with greater resilience and legitimacy. Testimonials from customers, experts, or media quotes can also provide further legitimacy. Third-party support is also valuable in sustaining the life of a meme, acting as a booster meme. The existence of an interested party behind a meme, with an evident reason to support and perpetuate its existence, may reassure potential targets.

When faced with a message featuring the views of an 'expert' you need to check his or her credibility. Is his or her expertise clearly defined? Is it relevant to the assignment? Is there a consensus among experts on the views he or she is expressing? Is there objective substantiation of the case?

Theresa Merrick of Glasgow Caledonian University is able to capitalize on the need for experts by using the knowledge of her university's academics – and also generate useful public relations for her institution:

> Most organizations have a lot of knowledge and know-how within their walls. As a university we obviously have a tremendous resource which we seek to create and capitalize on media opportunities wherever possible. Putting up an expert for the media to talk to generates good visibility and name awareness for the university. It is a good personal development opportunity for our lecturers and also positions us as leaders in our specialist areas.

You can manipulate the context of your information to boost your legitimacy. In a debate where there are opposing views, mentioning the opposition's arguments could indicate you are objective and fair, so enhancing your perceived trustworthiness. This tactic can be counter-productive if suggesting the existence of alternative views infers that the issue is actually controversial. Research shows that the more informed an audience is, the less likely it is to be persuaded by one-sided arguments, as people are already likely to know some counter-arguments.

Packing lots of information into your communication, creating message-dense communication, can cause confusion. A good example of this is the limitations of comparative advertising. This tactic is rarely used by a brand leader – you do not get Coca-Cola mentioning the number two brand Pepsi.

Dramatic difference

Any proposition should spell out the dramatic difference the user will gain as a result of your benefits. This stage binds the benefits you offer to your target's situation. A useful tip is to create dramatic differences for different levels of needs. Using Maslow's hierarchy of needs (1954), the dramatic differences for reading this book could include messages such as:

- Self actualization: 'Reading this book will fulfil your potential, both as a person and as a professional communicator.'
- Aesthetic needs: 'Reading this book will transform your understanding of how you communicate.'
- Cognitive needs: 'Reading this book will equip you with the latest ideas, processes and ways of doing to transform your communications.'
- Esteem needs: 'Reading this book will get you recognized as a great communicator.'
- Belongingness and love: 'Reading this book will enable you to be part of a new breed of communications professional extending the boundaries of public relations practice.'
- Safety needs: 'Reading this book will enable you to achieve greater results in your communications to give you an outstanding competitive edge.'
- Physiological needs: 'Reading this book will boost your earning power.'

Task: putting it into practice

How can you apply Maslow's hierarchy of needs to describe the benefits you or your organization offer? Review a recent communication. What different needs levels were addressed in it?

USE POINTS OF INFLUENCE

Individual communicators can skilfully tailor their message to harness key trigger points to get targets to respond. Cialdini in his seminal work *Influence* (2001) highlights a number of key triggers:

Reciprocation

This is the idea that one person must want to repay, in kind, what another person has provided. Introducing the element of obligation impels the recipient to return the favour at some point in the future. If you give something before asking for a return favour, it can lead people to agree to a request substantially larger than the gift they received. An alternative tactic is to make a large, usually unreasonable request. This could stimulate a reciprocation of concessions, where people might feel bad about making their initial refusal.

Commitment and consistency

Most people seek to be consistent in their words, beliefs, attitudes and deeds. It provides a short-cut to having to review and repeatedly redecide. If you secure an initial commitment people subsequently respond along the same lines. One ethically dubious technique used by salespeople is to get their prospect to answer 'yes' to a series of agreeable questions. When they then make their sales close, the prospect is more likely to then say 'Yes'.

Social proof

How something looks to other people can induce people to comply. If your actions can enable you to gain wider respect, it might encourage you to comply with a request. This 'keeping up with the Joneses' technique is often used at charity dinners to shame people into making a donation by not wishing to appear mean in front of other guests.

Liking

People prefer to say 'yes' to others they know and like. This homophily includes physical attractiveness, similarities with ourselves, and positive association, or anchoring, with things of mutual interest or respect. The quality of being likeable is an outstanding asset. If your audience likes you, they will forgive just about everything else you do wrong. If they don't like you, you can say the right things but it will not matter.

Authority

Everyone has strong pressures to conform and seek compliance with authority. Mere symbols of authority can be used to secure deference or obedience.

Scarcity

People assign more value to opportunities when they appear to be not readily available. Messages such as 'sale must end', or 'limited offer' are used extensively. Scarcity works because it boosts the perceived value, and we respond to any perceived loss of freedom by wanting to have the unobtainable item even more.

When they want someone to make a decision, most people tend to highlight the importance of their message but overlook emphasizing the urgency of the need to take action. People act when a need is perceived as both important and urgent.

Instant decisions

Making a decision on the basis of a single, perceived-to-be-reliable piece of information is particularly important in the context of the age of information overload. It emphasizes the growing importance of icon management in modern-day communications such as 'You can trust this person because ....'

Fear

Creating fear appeals can be powerful because they channel thoughts away from careful consideration and towards ridding yourself of the fear. This tactic actually works better with people who have high self-regard. They are more likely to be moved by fear such as from smoking. People with low self-regard have difficulty coping with threats to them, probably because they have a greater degree of permanent and pervasive pessimism regarding their abilities to take responsibility for their own destiny.

Fear is effective when:

● it scares people;
● it offers a specific recommendation for overcoming the cause of the fear;
● it comes with a recommended remedial action that is seen as credible;
● message recipients believe they can perform the recommended action.

Vividness

Vivid appeals can be emotionally interesting and so attract our feelings. Use of concrete, provocative images can stimulate an immediate response if they are able to connect the issue with matters personally close to us. Animal rights groups for example, often make use of shock images.

Vividness works because it attracts attention, and makes information more concrete and personal, so making the material more memorable. Its direct nature focuses thought on issues and arguments that people feel are most important.

People are deeply influenced by one clear, vivid personal example rather than by an abundance of statistics. As Joseph Stalin clinically observed, 'The death of a single Russian solider is a tragedy. A million deaths is a statistic ' (quoted in Nisbett and Ross, 1980).

Simon Collister, the former education officer of UK-based charity Epilepsy Action, emphasizes the importance of engaging people through using real-life drama: 'People relate to people; the more you can tell real stories about real people, the more likely others will listen and engage with you.'

Task: putting it into practice

Reflect on any recent negotiations you were involved with. Did you use any of these points of influence? Could you have used them in a different way?

BRIOCASTING: COMMUNICATE WITH FLAIR AND FLOURISH

A definition of 'briocasting' is to communicate with flair and flourish, to use your talents to engage your target audience in your message. What can you employ to transform what might seem dull, mundane or trivial? Elements for creating brio in your communications include:

- wow factor;
- active tense;
- metaphors.

The 'wow' factor

In your life you will have experiences which leave you thinking, 'Wow, that was good.' A 'wow' is characterized by:

- adding significance in some way to your life;
- being personal, something that makes you feel good about yourself;
- being unexpected: the 'wow' takes full advantage of the element of surprise.

A 'wow' does not necessarily have to be something extravagant or outrageous. Archie Norman MP, the former chair of superstore group Asda plc, tells the story of a visit he once made to an Irish supermarket. On taking his supermarket trolley at the shop entrance he was stopped by the store's greeter who welcomes shoppers. 'Oh, you've got a Brussels sprout leaf in your trolley, let me take it out for you.' Greatly impressed by this personal touch, he recounted the episode to the supermarket's owner only to be told: 'That's just Bernard's Brussels sprout leaf. He puts it in every trolley before you get there!' The greeter evidently discreetly replaces the leaf in the trolley to give him an excuse to demonstrate an act of courtesy. A 'wow' for a hardened supermarketeer – for the price of a Brussels sprout leaf.

Research shows that people leave bigger tips in restaurants when mints are left with the bill. Even bigger tips are left when the waiters make a point of providing extra mints, for their 'extra good customers' (Lynn, nd).

Active and passive tense

You should use language tense to manage your communications. The active tense should be used to involve people in what you say, engage them in the experience and stimulate passion and activity. In contrast you should use the passive to defuse the energy in a room and detach people from an experience. The passive tense is used in sentences like:

> One can make pictures mentally.
> Pictures can be made mentally.

These are the active versions:

> You can make pictures mentally.
> Make mental pictures – now.

Ideally you will have a rich and varied vocabulary to provide you with greater options. But please, although words can be important, do not get too hung up on the words you use in your communications. The best messages flow freely and naturally, and from the heart. And avoid jargon.

Metaphors

If a picture can paint a thousand words, a metaphor can deliver a million bayonets. Metaphors are one of the most powerful tools to use in communications. Martin Luther King did not say, 'I have a plan to improve the position of black people in society with a 10 per cent improvement each year.' He had a dream. Winston Churchill did not rouse the British people with details of the logistics in defending against any invading German forces. He would fight them on the beaches. These are examples of powerful metaphors at work.

A metaphor is any message that can be interpreted on a number of levels. Metaphors act like symbols as they provide a quick way to say a lot. When you choose a metaphor to describe your life or your situation, you choose the beliefs it supports too. Metaphors can be used to help people see, hear or feel the experience, help them understand information quicker, and make them feel different about the subject matter.

Metaphors work by:

- gaining attention;
- simplifying information;
- touching emotions;
- being memorable;
- working on multiple levels;
- allowing each of us our own interpretation.

In communications each of us puts up barriers to prevent messages getting through. It may be you may lack understanding of a subject, or want to avoid something which might cause dissonance or require you to make a change of behaviour. Let us use a metaphor to explain metaphors. Imagine you are playing cricket. The bowler bowls the ball to you, and you could hit the ball for six. Imagine however, if before the ball gets to you, instead of just one ball it divides into two, three or more different balls. You might be able to hit one of the balls, or even two, but potentially one of the balls can get past your defences and hit the wicket. A metaphor not only gets past defences, but can also gain leverage by impacting on your values system.

Indeed, for communications to change behaviour metaphors are the most powerful tool. An example from my own work in running a public relations consultancy demonstrates the power of metaphors to change behaviours. My firm entertains key contacts at a number of business dinners each year. I would wholeheartedly agree with the statement that clients are the most important group to a business. However my behaviour did not match this statement. In reality I tended to invite prospective clients ahead of existing clients, as part of the company's marketing efforts. Fortunately I was told this story.

A man facing the prospect of death had the opportunity to visit Heaven and Hell so he could decide where to spend his afterlife. On visiting heaven he reflected how decent, civilized and pleasant everything was, and thought he wouldn't mind coming there. On visiting Hell he was treated to a feast of hedonistic indulgence, a fantastic party. So when the fateful day came and he left this world, he made the decision to go to Hell. On arrival he was taken down a dark dank corridor into a foul cellar with only water and a few crumbs to sate his hunger. After a few days he had had enough, so he went to the Devil and remonstrated, 'Before I came for good I was treated fantastically, but now this is real purgatory. What's happened?' The Devil replied: 'Before you were a prospect; now you're a client.'

This story persuaded me that existing clients should be the first people to be invited to events. Prospective clients are only considered after the clients. A metaphor changed my behaviour.

Task: putting it into practice

Review your use of metaphors in your recent communications. What metaphors would you use to describe yourself? Draw up a list of your all-time favourite metaphors used in any communications campaigns.

MAKE YOUR MESSAGE BESPOKE

The more you can make your communications suited to the preferences of your target, the more effective they will be. Two key objectives in selling your message are to take into account your target's personality profile and his or her preferred thinking style.

Personality profiles

Everyone on this planet is an individual, with a unique personality. In the same way that you can divide the human race up into men/women, tall/short, black/white, blonde/dark hair and so on, you can divide them into categories of preferred decision-making style. There tends to be distinct styles in how people make decisions, and also in how they prefer to use and manage information. If you can identify the preferred decision-making style of your target, you can then tailor your material to meet his or her needs.

There are numerous established personality profiling systems in common circulation. A useful model for public relations practitioners uses four groups defined by which of four symbols they choose, as shown in Figure 6.2 (taken from Green, 2001).

Figure 6.2 *Personality profiles*

Triangle △

Like the symbol, these people are characterized by a clear sense of direction. Rather like an arrowhead speeding through space, they are more ambitious than most, setting clear targets in life and working towards them with single-minded dedication. They tend to be natural leaders, and perhaps workaholics, sacrificing family and friends in eagerness to achieve goals.

Square □

The most logical symbol, with four right angles, the square is chosen by equally logical people. They prefer facts and figures rather than guesswork when solving problems or reaching decisions. They dislike hunches and distrust intuition, instead assessing challenging situations objectively rather than emotionally.

Squiggle $\mathcal{S}$

This tends to be chosen by people who take a more off-beat view of life. They have boundless energy and enthusiasm coupled with a need to become involved in a wide range of activities. They hate routine, loathe being pinned down and are at their best when able to enjoy plenty of variety.

Circle ◯

This is the most harmonious symbol. People who choose this are skilled at dealing with other people, with their warmth and understanding putting others quickly at ease. They have strong empathic skills and are sensitive to the needs of other people, knowing intuitively how others feel and having the ability to respond in the most appropriate way.

Visual issues

People take in information using many different sensory channels. Some like to see materials or demonstrations of your argument. Others are primarily auditory, liking to hear the communication. Others still are kinaesthetic. These people gain information by doing and experiencing. If you identify the preferred sensory style of your target you can tailor the appropriate style of presentation. If you are dealing with groups you will do best to cover all three types in your actions and words; in pictures, sounds, and in feelings.

TOOLS FOR DIFFERENT SENSORY CHANNELS

Visuals

Be seen. Use illustrations, colour, graphs and gestures. Your language should correspond, using phrases such as 'I see', 'What does this look like?' and 'Do you get the picture?'

Auditory

Make sure you are heard. Use a variety of tones in your voice, slow down the pace of your speech, and use different sounds. Include phrases such as 'I hear what you say', 'That sounds good' and 'It's got a good ring to it.'

Kinaesthetic

Offer opportunities to move and feel. Provide handouts so people can handle the material. Phrases to employ include 'How do you feel about this?', 'I've got a handle on this' and 'How does this grab you?'

Task: putting it into practice

What is your personality profile? What are the profiles of key individuals you need to communicate with? What different ways could you tailor your message to suit their personality profile or preferred thinking style? How effective could this understanding of individual styles be when you next have to negotiate, or manage a conflict or relationship?

COMMUNICATE FOR OTHERS TO CHANGE BEHAVIOUR OR TO GET THEM TO ACT

Much public relations communications fails because it assumes that if you just give people information they will then be in a position to make their minds up, and this, it is hoped, will lead them to act in your favour. Outstanding communicators not only ensure their message gets through and is remembered, they also ensure, by using a variety of tactics, that they trigger their message to lead the target to take action.

PR FUTURES DEBATE

Should public relations managers be in charge of managing their organization's metaphors?

PERSONAL CHECKLIST

- What are the benefits you personally provide to your stakeholders?
- How do you legitimize your status in your work?
- What dramatic difference do you make in your work?
- Do you really work back from your target audiences when you communicate or do you just tell them what you want to?
- How many call to action tools do you use in your communications?

- Is there a 'wow' in your communications?
- Do you, like the great Greek orator, use metaphors in your work?
- Do you, like a miner's wife, capitalize on the emotional dimension to your message?
- Listen to speeches and pay attention to the use of metaphors.
- What are the personality profiles of your boss, your partner or key targets?

PRELUDE TO CHAPTER 7

Word-of-mouth (w-o-m) is the most potent form of communication – pass it on. W-o-m is perhaps one of the most powerful tools for marketing communications thanks its credibility, its coming from trusted sources and its ability to replicate like wildfire. W-o-m does not just happen but can be proactively instigated, stimulated, stretched and boosted to reach many different audiences.

Online communications can also transform your ability to communicate quickly and with many different people to speedily build a critical mass. You need to be aware of the practical limitations of online tools and how they operate in a rapidly changing environment. In this new age of communications everyone can have their 15 minutes of fame, or be a 'nonebrity'.

7

Adapting your messages to your networks – word-of-mouth and word-of-click, your viral friends

There are many heads of public relations, communications, marketing and advertising, but have you ever met a 'head of word of mouth'? Why? Because most believe word of mouth (w-o-m) is something that cannot be directly managed. It is seen as a phenomenon out of control, beyond people's reach. That's wrong. W-o-m should be recognized as a marketing communications discipline, under the aegis of public relations, which can be planned, managed and integrated into a wider communications strategy. Creating messages which are w-o-m friendly and managing the w-o-m dimension are among the key characteristics of the outstanding public relations communicator.

Every great communicator, whether he or she is a leader, politician or public relations practitioner, usually has a phrase or series of messages associated with him or her. The ones whose legend grows long after their death are the ones with the best soundbites, in fields from literature, such as Oscar Wilde – 'I have nothing to declare except my genius' (www. brainyquote.com) – to sport, such as the former Liverpool football club manager Bill Shankly, who reflected 'Some people believe football is a matter of life and death. I'm very disappointed with that attitude. I can assure you it is much, much more important than that' (www.shankly. com).

WHAT IS W-O-M?

W-o-m is essentially about circulating messages and memes relevant to your future success which enable other people to communicate about you. It can be defined as communication whose content and source is perceived as independent. It is this independence of w-o-m, with its unique credibility, along with its meme-like ability to replicate and become self-sustaining, that gives it so much power.

Many public relations practitioners are guilty of failing to recognize the third dimension in their communications. They effectively plan their messages to target audiences but give little thought to the sustainability of the memes created in the communications. Communicators need to adopt what can be called '3D thinking'. Most focus their communications efforts in just two dimensions: first, on their outputs in broadcasting a message, and second, on achieving outcomes from reaching target audiences. The third dimension focuses on the next stage in the communications process – outgrowths, particularly the subsequent relaying or outcasting of w-o-m messages, or memes, to further audiences, where the message develops its own dynamic beyond the sender and the recipient.

Think back to any recent press release or campaign. What is the key thing, summarized in one or two sentences, that captures the essence of your message? If you cannot articulate this soundbite message how can you expect others to pass it on?

THE POWER OF W-O-M

Most people rate w-o-m as their most potent source of new business or reliable information. You know the scene: you are making a choice or dealing with an unfamiliar problem. You are not sure what to do. It could be a major purchase, or even just deciding what film to see. You ask a friend, or the friend tells you, 'It's supposed to be good.' This recommendation probably determines your decision.

What gives w-o-m most of its power is that it offers legitimacy in the message by harnessing someone else's experience. Somebody else is paying the bill in time, cost or risk. Harnessing his or her experience reduces your potential dissonance, and lessens the anxiety felt in making a purchase or decision.

Lack of a direct, positive experience is usually the single greatest factor holding back any decision from greater and faster acceptance. To learn the lesson of emergence theory, the smaller the step you have to take in a decision, the more likely you will take it.

People don't buy the best; they buy the least risk. That last sentence is so important it needs to be repeated: *people don't buy the best; they buy the least risk.* The VHS video format for example, although technically inferior to its Betamax and V2000 rivals, became the industry standard because JVC made its system open and thus secured wider availability. People consequentially chose VHS because it was perceived to be less of a risk. Think of the last time you drove a long distance and stopped at a branded national chain of diners. You knew exactly what you would be getting in terms of service, food and experience, and chose that rather than risk a roadside independent café, which might have been a far more rewarding experience, but on the other hand might have been disappointing. The choice, or product, which it is easiest to decide on wins – not the best.

W-o-m is custom tailored to the audience. You do not get bombarded with recommendations from a trusted source because people do not recommend things unless they think you are potentially interested. You subsequently pay more attention to the w-o-m recommendation because it is perceived to be more relevant, and more complete, than any other form of communication.

In the age of the information explosion ironically your targets can hardly hear you. A modern-day copy of the *Financial Times* contains more information than the average person in 17th-century Britain would have come across in a lifetime. Nowadays, we are typically exposed to 1,500 ads daily. You are deluged with useless information. There has been more telephone traffic in the last seven years than in the previous 70 years. People protect themselves from this overload by filtering out most messages. They do however listen to their friends, or other trusted contacts, through w-o-m.

W-o-m is also self-generating. The replicating nature of memes provides a self-propelling message – you hear something which you then tell someone, who in turn tells someone else. The population of the UK can be reached by 10 people telling 10 people, and just repeating this process six times.

115

Deborah Heindley has an outstanding track record in tourism promotion. W-o-m is one of her most powerful tools:

> Any time I have promoted a new venue it is vital to try and get as many word of mouth going by getting as many people as possible to sample, experience and see at first hand the venue by enticing them in with special promotions, tie-ins with other partners, and any links. If you have got a good product, offer a memorable experience. They will tell their friends, family, neighbours, work colleagues and do your promotional job for you.

Task: putting it into practice

What is your personal w-o-m? What do others say about you? What new w-o-m messages can you create about yourself? What memorable quote can you create about you or your brand?

NEGATIVE W-O-M

Often w-o-m can be negative. There is nothing that cannot be made worse in the telling! The perceived wisdom is that people are ten times more likely to tell others about a negative experience than a positive one. Positive experiences are expected, and soon forgotten, whereas negative situations get people frustrated and angry, consequently energizing their output of negative w-o-m. This impetus is generated by negative experiences creating dissonance anxiety within the aggrieved person. Dishing out negative w-o-m, or just plain simple badmouthing, helps lessen the feeling of dissonance. It is a form of getting your own back and makes you feel better in the process.

In managing negative w-o-m you can harness this reality in a constructive way. Providing some negatives in your communications can be more reassuring than simply including positives. The negatives can add credibility to your message, providing an 'inoculation effect'. (I once had a meeting with a representative from McDonald's restaurants, who swiftly said, 'Before we start I just want to get some things clear. We don't make our burgers from plastic.' She went on to list a couple of other publicized negatives about the company. She said all this without it seemed drawing breath, and then concluded, 'Now what is it we're meeting about today?') (See also 'inoculation theory' in Chapter 10.)

Competitors can also spread a negative buzz. There are some hair-raising tales about the energy industry in the 19th century using negative public relations and w-o-m. Thomas Edison initially found himself the victim when the gas industry, threatened by the advent of his electric lighting, belittled the significance and exaggerated the dangers of this newfangled electricity. The roles were reversed when Edison later used even more outrageous tricks against George Westinghouse's competing alternating current system. Edison resorted to showing newspaper reporters macabre executions of stray cats and dogs by alternating current. Edison even persuaded the state of New York in 1888 to switch from hanging to electrocution by alternating current as its official form of execution!

Using any form of negative w-o-m, or badmouthing the competition, should carry a strong health warning. It can be highly counter-productive, with people feeling sympathy for the target of the abuse, and can also lower your own esteem with the prospect. As my grandmother used to advise, 'If you can't say anything nice about people, don't say anything at all.' It is still a good principle to live your life by.

Dissatisfied customers can not only be neutralized by having their immediate problem solved, but also be completely turned around to become advocates extolling the virtues of your legendary customer service. The story of how the US retailer Nordstrom dealt with the customer who demanded and received a refund for a tyre – even though Nordstrom did not sell tyres – is a powerful w-o-m legend.

To avoid negative w-o-m the fundamental lesson is if you make a mistake, correct it immediately. Positively responding to complaints creates a culture focused on the customer. Fundamentally do not think of complainers as pests, but ask yourself why do they feel this way and see them as potential allies. If you are not talking in an open way with your customers, how will you be able to meet their changing needs? You need to examine what opportunities you are creating for customer dialogue.

Task: putting it into practice

What negative w-o-m exists about you? What do others tell about you? What can you do to counter this?

LIMITATIONS OF W-O-M

If w-o-m is so powerful why is it not more effectively used and managed? It does have its limitations. It is uncontrolled. Rather like the football manager who cannot guarantee a result, the end product of w-o-m is outside your hands. What the good w-o-m manager can do is shape all the factors to help in communications, but ultimately the final power to connect rests beyond his or her direct grasp.

W-o-m takes time, for people to accumulate enough favourable experiences, and to subsequently communicate them. The saliency of the topic – how importantly the subject is perceived by you or the target, and how frequently the product is used or purchased – will influence the extent and nature of your w-o-m. If the contact or purchase is infrequent, there is the problem of w-o-m not being sustained during the intervening periods.

The source of the w-o-m is crucial. Initial stages of w-o-m are sustained by people who are influencers, able to impart their qualified information to wider groups. Rather like trying to light a wet bonfire, the hardest part of w-o-m can be to get the buzz going in the first place.

Only in rare cases does a buzz spread like wildfire. There is always someone who wants to keep the word from spreading. Opposing groups with their own blocker memes can restrict the w-o-m meme. Buzz is often generated about new things, and new things always threaten someone. Also, products may be well established or lack any perceived interest to stimulate w-o-m. Even within w-o-m networks there is a potential information overload. People do not always listen or act. A strong w-o-m message in one network may be difficult to move from one cluster to another. Limited, or no, management of the w-o-m dimension accentuates these shortcomings.

HOW CAN YOU MANAGE W-O-M?

Do you or your organization have one distinguishing feature that potential targets are aware of? Do you get your target audiences thinking about themselves in a way makes it impossible not to call you? All these are potentially manageable elements.

Your current w-o-m

As with any communications strategy, you need to identify where you are at present. Auditing your w-o-m is based on listening to your networks, knowing what your audiences are saying and using all possible approaches to hear what 'buzz' there is about you.

A useful tool for public relations practitioners is to profile their w-o-m, perhaps using a scale like this:

–4 **High-level negative w-o-m.** People actively dissuade. Examples can be taboo subjects such as hard drugs and child abuse.

–3 **Unprompted strong negative w-o-m.** Highly active negative w-o-m where people go out of their way to provide negative comment about someone, with their full personal endorsement and authority behind it.

–2 **Prompted negative w-o-m.** A strong reaction to an issue, product or service. When faced with this situation a 'keep your head' down strategy should be avoided, where any proactive communications can stimulate unarticulated, negative w-o-m.

–1 **Relative prompted negative w-o-m.** Although dissatisfied people do not go out of their way to badmouth the brand, and even use or buy it sometimes, perhaps through lack of alternatives, despite their negative disposition.

0 **Neutral, little good or bad w-o-m**. The 'it's awright factor' where people are broadly impassive to the issue, product or service.

1 **Relative positive prompted w-o-m.** People have nice things to say but require prompting to be aware of, or reveal, them. Conventional communications can trigger and raise this type of w-o-m to boost to the next level.

2 **Prompted positive w-o-m.** When asked, people rave, offering a highly positive testimonial and endorsement. Typically, conventional communications tends to reinforce rather than engage this asset, with little use of 'tell your friends now' type messages.

3 **Unprompted positive w-o-m.** People go out of their way to convince others.

4 **High-level positive w-o-m.** An outstanding positive advocate, people go out of their way to provide constructive feedback. There is a danger of managing expectations where your reality cannot keep up with the target's fanaticism.

In examining your w-o-m activities you need to consider what you are doing to support your unprompted positive w-o-m advocates to help them spread your word, while any negative w-o-m should be neutralized or transformed. Also, what w-o-m are you using not only to help your targets adopt your message, but also to speed up their decision-making?

IDENTIFYING THE IMPORTANT AND URGENT

Different products or situations will influence the potential for w-o-m. Ideally, products or services need to be:

● compelling: people want to try them;
● easy to try without risk;
● visible to potential users.

A w-o-m buzz has a different impact on different types of business. The w-o-m potential of a situation will be determined by a number of 'contagious attributes'. It works well when there is:

- High involvement among customers, where the idea, product, or service has high potential conversation value.
- Excitement in some way in the product.
- Innovation and something genuinely new about the product or service.
- A personal experience, for example hotels, cars, airlines and restaurants.
- A complex product, where there is a need to reduce risk.
- A high-level of risk or expense involved in a choice. If the subject is 'mission critical' it will be adopted more carefully. If it is expensive, again there is a high need to reduce risk and dissonance.
- Observable, such as clothes, mobile phones and cars. People are less likely to discuss a product if it is 'invisible'. How would you, for example, describe your own pension plan?
- Offering social validation involved by making the purchase, such as the places which people perceive as defining their lifestyle or status in your network or community.
- A promoter behind the w-o-m who has sufficient energy and critical mass to make substantive connections.
- A high perceived credibility of subject matter among target audiences.

Different factors influence the potential w-o-m capability of a situation. The emotional involvement with a product is a good predictor of how many people will subsequently be told about experience with it. Cars have a high emotional interest and create an emotional bond with their users; most people can remember every car they have had, many can talk about the subject for hours, and lots of people see what car people drive as a sign of their material success and a lifestyle statement.

The privacy factor will also affect potential w-o-m. Fewer people will talk and tell about their own personal financial position and specific use of services. Healthcare is another potential area where discretion and the desire of people to keep their personal life private can hinder the w-o-m dynamic.

David Taylor is a successful lifestyle coach with a track record of working with leading figures in business and public life. A frustration he experiences, however, is that his clients are most reluctant to admit they use the services of a life coach:

> Despite achieving a real difference in helping my clients get the most from themselves and the opportunities they face, people often regard their using a life coach perhaps as a sign of weakness. As a result, unlike other businesses, it is rare I get a direct referral from a satisfied customer.

In the UK, the National Health Service (NHS) is regularly criticized in the media, creating the impression that the service is on the verge of collapse or significantly under-performing. Yet day in, day out, the NHS successfully treats thousands of patients and provides a relatively good performance. It clearly is failing to harness the power of positive w-o-m. The 1.2 million NHS staff should be trained to encourage their satisfied patients to spread the word about their experience.

W-o-m will spread more significantly and extensively if there is a:

- Crisis – where people's own individual well-being could be perceived to be at risk.
- Mission – the need for concerted effort to accomplish a major goal.
- Problem – rapid involvement of many people desirable to solve the challenge.
- Danger – where spreading the message about a potential danger can significantly increase the safety of each person. This operates as a result of reciprocal altruism. The act might evidently appear altruistic, in that people are doing something for the benefit of others. It can be rationalized as furthering their self-interest in the hope others would do the same thing for them in similar circumstances.

IDENTIFYING THE CRUCIAL STAGES IN MAKING A DECISION

When faced with a decision there are four major phases people go through:

- Information stage – they cast around, sourcing data to establish their available options.
- Verification stage – they try to find confirmatory evidence to discover if their information is true, they decide to decide, and ultimately select from among their options.
- Implementation/ongoing use stage – their feedback from trial determines whether they abandon the choice or expand their commitment.
- Advocacy stage (both negative or positive) – they decide to go beyond neutral to either positive or negative advocacy in their w-o-m.

The need for w-o-m information will also depend on the relationship between the w-o-m sender and receiver. These relationships can be characterized as either expert to expert, where information is more important than verification; or expert to non-expert, where w-o-m confirmation and verification are more important than information.

Each of the above networks will require different w-o-m seeding in both content and in the initial dissemination of the message. Different audiences will vary in their needs and also have a different propensity to spread w-o-m. Immigrant groups for example may rely on peers or community leaders. Age may have an impact, with young people, for example, being more influenced by peers than by the media.

The more specifically you tailor your w-o-m messages to the relevant stage in the decision-making process, the more effective they will be. In the information stage accuracy and availability of information is crucial. At the verification stage third-party testimonials and case studies can be used to provide confirmatory evidence.

Different w-o-m strategies work in different parts of the adoption of ideas or products cycle. They can be used to not only secure positive w-o-m but also speed up the decision-making process.

IDENTIFYING WHAT 'STICKY' WORDS ARE NEEDED TO ACCELERATE EACH PROBLEMATIC STEP

For successful w-o-m communications your message has to 'be sticky' – a coherent and easily copyable meme. It has to be memorable and attractive to your audience. Your message has to be clearly stated, challenging yet achievable, and most importantly, excite the prospect to engage, motivate and inspire to action.

For successful w-o-m you need a 'story'. The story needs to be:

- short and simple;
- interesting, exciting, new, different, unique, worth talking about;
- in story form.

Seth Godin (2002) emphasizes the importance in any successful w-o-m, or idea virus, of 'smoothness': how easy is it for an end user to spread particular messages. In shaping your messages to boost their smoothness, potentially strong angles to be exploited include:

- News: genuine newness will be of interest. (Note, it does have to be genuinely new and not just a tired reformulation of the old.)
- Unique results, effects or activities, appealing to 'What's in it for me?'
- Sex – a core human motivator.
- Secrets – capitalizing on the scarcity rule.
- Helping others – appealing to curiosity and reciprocal altruism.

- The 'Fortean factor' – how unusual, odd or different is it to your target's normal experience.
- Personal – 'legends' of exceptional performance are more attractive than statistics. Give people a hero to identify and connect with, as any buzz spreads faster when it involves a person, because people closely associate with other people.
- Celebrity linkage – using a well-known personality to provide further brand coherence to your message.

IDENTIFYING DIFFERENT WAYS TO DELIVER YOUR W-O-M

W-o-m does not just happen, but can be created, instigated, shaped and extended by a variety of tactics including the following.

Sampling

If someone has direct experience of you, your message or product they can see at first hand what you are like, and reduce any future dissonance in deciding to buy or use you. You are creating a half-step decision for them. Also, by giving something you are invoking reciprocity – your target has a sense of owing you something in return.

The concept of 'samples' can include a free consultation, articles, free delivery or low-cost workshops. How much does your website educate prospects and tell them about themselves?

When 3M launched the Post-it note it initially found sales disappointing. Only in test markets where extensive free sampling had been used did sales skyrocket. The Post-It was a new concept, meeting an unarticulated need. People had to use it before they could readily appreciate its benefits. What 'sample gaps' are there in your communications?

Seeding

This too can be used to accelerate the rate of w-o-m. Targeting innovators and adopters with special offers helps speed up the rate of adoption, in contrast to waiting for nature to take its course. Seeding at strategic points stimulates further take-up within networks.

Seed target special offers can include targeted discount offers, loans and free samples. A car manufacturer for example might find it made sense to lend cars to influential individuals, as people might not notice a new television commercial, but they will notice their neighbour with a new car.

Seeding is not a new concept. Whether it was opera singers hiring people in the audience to cheer 'Bravo', or the trick the author witnessed in East End street markets of a market trader having one or two plants in the audience who are the first to buy and encourage the others to similarly make a purchase, the seeds act as the trigger for the rest to follow.

Showmanship and the use of unconventional methods can provoke or accentuate w-o-m. Outlandish guarantees, wild offers, outrageous trials and stunts can stimulate interest and subsequent buzz.

Sourcing

Many potential customers are not connected to existing channels. You need to reach people where they hang out. Illegal recreational drugs is one of the largest business sectors in the UK. It evidently does not spend a penny on formal advertising and relies on w-o-m.

It is possible to combine many of the above elements, as Mark Borkowski, a leading practitioner in the field of creating buzz, recalls:

> For one client we devised a milk float drop targeted at celebrities where we found out where they lived and delivered product samples with their morning milk delivery. It's about creating curiosity and getting it talked about.

WORD-OF-CLICK

I saw my first fax machine in 1983, typed my first document on a word processor in 1986, first used a mobile phone in 1989, got connected to the internet and sent my first e-mail in 1996. I had my first website in 1997, and cannot seemingly function now as a communicator without any of these tools. Do new ways of reaching people really change the way you communicate?

One of the most successful sectors to exploit the commercial potential of the internet is the pornography industry. One of the world's oldest surviving advertisements, over 2,000 years old, can be found at the ancient site of Ephesus in Turkey. It promotes a brothel.

Any classicist will tell you that people over the centuries have not fundamentally changed their core motives and desires. Rumours of the death of the written word are also greatly exaggerated, with the widespread use of text messages and e-mails. Yet new forms of communication are providing new dimensions to w-o-m activities.

HYPER SELF-PERPETUITY

E-communications can be likened to 'word of mouth communications on steroids'. The pre-internet era restricted w-o-m to close circles of peers, colleagues, friends and family. E-mails offer a new ball game. A typical online user has a 25 to 50-person mailing list. Word-of-click (w-o-c) acts in the same way as w-o-m marketing, creating an information virus which can tap into people's existing networks, allowing them to take advantage of existing trusting relationships.

A buzz on the internet travels faster because it combines local and non-local networks, using technology that allows instant communications on a multiple scale. Unlike traditional w-o-m, working on a linear route with one person telling another who tells another, e-communications can work on a number of multi-parallel connections, all of whom potentially can broadcast your message, like a machine-gun firing, to many new targets. This makes the whole communication process quicker and also more capable of creating significant critical mass within a short space of time.

If a viral w-o-c message is circulating in a network it offers the opportunity for a target to be reached from several different sources. This can provide endorsement for the credibility of the message – the 'if so many different people are in on this, it must be good' factor – coupled with the advantage of being able to remind the target with repeat messages. Research in selling reveals that it requires up to seven quality contacts before a salesperson successfully lands the sale. Receiving multiple e-mails from different sources can mimic this process.

HYPER-FAST: SPEED AND IMMEDIACY

The 21st century can be characterized as the 'amber-less generation'. Imagine a set of traffic lights without the amber segment in the changing light sequence. The amber light gives the motorist time to think and prepare. Communications have been given the facility to move faster. They have also been denied the breathing space to think and prepare.

Organizations tend to focus their attention on managing the dimensions of cost and quality. Yet the dimension of time will be increasingly crucial for future success for general business management and the effective communicator. The goalposts in using communications have moved with the ability to communicate quicker. Equally people's expectations of faster responses have also increased. People can be reached quicker. They expect answers quicker – if not from you, then they will get them from someone else.

We live in an age of liquid modernity – a fluidness extending to every aspect of life. The rapid speed of communications means you can be more vulnerable to other people and their memes stealing your share of space in your prospects' minds.

HYPER-AVAILABILITY AND INFORMATION OBESITY

George Orwell got it wrong in *1984* when he envisaged the means of control of the masses through the all-seeing Big Brother. He had not envisaged the rise of the middle classes, who on the whole, actively seek methods of control such as closed-circuit television to monitor all that is going on.

The age of new communications means that you will never be out of touch, whether you like it or not. The experience of public relations consultant Ian Green is not atypical: 'I took a call from a journalist on my mobile phone – nothing unusual except I was in the middle of a walking holiday of Hadrian's Wall!'

While there has been an explosion in the wealth of opportunities for individuals to reach out and communicate, there is the limitation of the 'abundance communications paradox': the growth in the ability to communicate has been matched by a rise in the immunity to communications. Remember the first e-mail you got? You probably sent a long and eloquent reply. Now with the explosive growth in e-mail communications, you develop response strategies to limit your overload to enable you to cope and respond to what you perceive as the crucial messages. You use spam filters, delete e-mails without reading or with no reply. When you do reply it is often short – often several days/weeks later, an ironic time lag in an age of instant communications.

Prospective targets can hardly hear you. People protect themselves by filtering out most messages. They do listen however to their friends or known contacts. Prospective targets will also find ways to seek you out, as Adrian Mahoney reveals:

> I absolutely hate phoning up complete strangers and trying to tout for business. Thanks to my website, I don't need to. My website outlines all my services and allows potential clients to check me out anonymously. If they don't like my tone – or what I'm offering – they'll go elsewhere. Likewise, if they're interested, they can fill out an online form and ask for more information. I've won lots of business this way. Thanks to this, and happy clients telling others about me, I don't cold call these days – I don't need to.

HYPER-DEMOCRATIC

The new era of communications is also witnessing the age of the 'non-ebrity', where people can be famous for no particular merit or ability; they are famous because they are famous. The explosion in media outlets, reality television and tabloids provides opportunities for communicators to create instant celebrity through mass media visibility or creating a viral buzz through online media.

HYPER-DISTORTION OF YOUR MESSAGE AND ACTIONS

The age of hyper-communications encourages greater polarity. Debates and arguments may be moderate in other media, but the need for hyper-fast responses polarizes an issue into clear black/white dimensions, creating more extreme views. E-communications also can distort the tenor and subtleties of communications. In one study people were found to hold dissenting opinions and expressed their arguments most frequently and persistently when online. It appears that the anonymity offered by online communications may encourage people to articulate more severe views than they would be ready to express in other contexts.

Expressing dissent is a lot harder in a face-to-face situation. It is easier through remote communications over the phone or in an e-mail. A key factor in the burnout of call centre staff is the level of abuse they face from irate customers. (As a trustee of my local theatre I was amazed to find out that even among the genteel ranks of theatregoers, the theatre box office experienced abusive 'phone rage' when people could not get the tickets they wanted.)

The spread of any memes you produce will be helped if they can suitably adapt to different media channels. Memes that are media cross-channel friendly will be stronger than those limited to single mediums.

VIRAL CAMPAIGN TACTICS

The first 'e-mail' was created by Ray Tomlinson in 1971 when he wrote the 200-line program that allowed a user to send a message to any computer hooked up to Arpanet, the forefather of the internet developed by the US Department of Defense. The strength of e-mail is that it can send multiple messages to any number of targets. The targets themselves can easily send on the message to new audiences. In theory this should be the ultimate communications tool. Its strength is also its weakness: the ease of sending out and sending on messages means it is easily available to everyone to do the same.

The first viral online campaign is reputed to be a 1994 student campaign against cuts in student grants at the University of North London. Since then the idea has emerged from the margins into an increasingly respectable marketing tool. Key elements to encourage and make it easy to be a link in viral online marketing are:

- Give new insight or knowledge by sending on content or samples of a product or service.
- Share content for fun, where you need to ensure the content is creative and engaging and merits passing on to a friend despite the lack of an explicit offer, such as jokes, spoofs, quizzes, tests and personality tests.
- Provide a communal good, whether it is an e-mail warning about the latest virus, or giving people the chance to win a competition or raise money for charity.
- Seeking a political good, such as asking people to sign up to a petition.
- Appealing to a sexual titillation or a superstitious fear through chain mail.

Adrian Mahoney of the PR Store is a great advocate of individual practitioners fully harnessing the opportunities of new media:

> Using e-mail effectively is one of the best ways to work smarter and more effectively. Used wisely it can also make you look just as important as large corporations. And that can give you a competitive edge when you run a small business. For starters, route your e-mail through a domain name (such as theprstore.net) to get that big-company persona. Domain names cost only a few pounds a year, and look so much better than sending out andy@verycheapisp.com. You can route your domain name to another e-mail address – even a web-based one like Hotmail; handy if you travel about a lot.

Here's an example of a viral campaign used by marketing expert John Grant with the author to promote his new book.

> Hi Andy
>
> You wrote to me after my article in the FT a few years back about your book on creativity in public relations. Now I'm writing to tell you I have a new book out next week – called After Image. I'm hoping you might help me in a little viral marketing ...

Here's the sting. If it looks interesting you might consider being my viral marketing friend by forwarding this note to five other people you know, who might appreciate the book. I'm only sending this note initially to 20 people around the world who contacted me through my first book. Who knows, if you all forward this note, and then they forward it too, maybe I'll have a case study for my next book!

What I'll offer in return is that anybody using a forwarded copy of this e-mail to write to me, can ask me anything they like about marketing, the book ... – I can't promise to 'know the answer' but I will reply to any e-mail I receive in this way. Given my usual consulting fees, I think that's fairly generous.

I hope this works and that some of you do go on to enjoy my new book!

Best wishes

John Grant

Task: putting it into practice

What different ways can you use a viral campaign to communicate? What can you get your key customers to say about you? What can you get new contacts to pass on about you?

AVOID EMBARRASSMENT – A WORD OF WARNING

An e-mail can be as private as a postcard. Claire Swire and Jo Moore must be two people who wish e-mail had not been invented. Ms Swire sent an e-mail to her boyfriend with explicit details of their private life. Her boyfriend chose to circulate this to his immediate circle of contacts, who in turn sent it on to their contacts. What was originally an intimate note became the online talk of the country. Jo Moore, an adviser to the then UK Transport Minister Stephen Byers, advised Labour MPs during the height of the events of 9/11 to immediately issue any bad news which would be buried in the fallout from the day's tragic story. There are not many seasoned public practitioners who, hand on heart, would not admit to the validity of the advice. Unfortunately for Ms Moore, the tone, language and timing of the e-mail proved disastrous for the careers of herself and her boss when it fell into the wrong hands.

The golden rule of e mail writing is to always ask yourself if you would be comfortable with your message being forwarded to others, especially to those who might want to use it against you.

Task: putting it into practice

Think about any e-mails you have received that you regarded as inappropriate. Have you issued any e-mails which are similarly unsuitable?

USING NET COMMUNITIES

Creating your own online net community can provide a forum for two-way communication to provide support, self-help and feedback for your cause. Users go to find out things, usually frequented by people who are the first to know and find any quick fixes. These communities can form an extended network, providing feedback and co-creation. Online communities, based around chat platforms where individuals with a shared interest can interact with each other, offer an ideal seedbed for a viral campaign.

Adrian Mahoney believes these net communities can greatly extend the capability of public relations communicators:

> Newsgroups or online groups can be a great way to meet people in particular communities. They can also expand your social life. Join a group and you might get asked to a useful networking seminar. Alternatively log onto big company websites and check out their free events. I once spotted something Microsoft was organizing. I signed up (online, of course). At the event I was able to buy discounted software (saving £400) and even signed up for another free networking event – where I was able to meet more (non-techie) business contacts.

Message boards, like informal chatroom message boards, offer a simple but highly visible opportunity to promote your content. Whereas chatrooms are active real-time environments, message boards offer a more passive forum for interaction. 'E-fluential' contacts are far more active users of e-mail, newsgroups and bulletin boards. You should assign your own time or colleagues to monitor forums and other internet discussions relevant for your activities.

The opportunities presented by w-o-m and w-o-c for the public relations communicator are bound to grow. Pass it on.

W-O-M: A PUBLIC RELATIONS DISCIPLINE?

W-o-m is a public relations discipline. It draws on the core strengths of public relations in using what your stakeholders think of you as the starting point for a dialogue. It uses your real reputation, not hype, to sustain its message. W-o-m, like public relations, depends on delivering a core truth. If your product is poor, no amount of public relations – or hype – is going to get people to buy it time and time again. W-o-m spans every stakeholder and is not a narrow, focused advertising tool. Formal w-o-m management is a new concept and presents an opportunity for the public relations industry to become the lead partners in managing this dimension to marketing communications.

PR people were the first viral marketers; they would send a message out to a third party, such as sending a press release to journalists, as part of a planned programme to gain wider currency and coverage. They used their skill and expertise to craft and shape the message to assist it gaining acceptance and use. They had no control over its ultimate take-up and use.

Which sector is taking the lead in the UK viral marketing market? When the internet first came on the scene in the 1990s it provided an opportunity since it offered a genuine two-way medium which was flexible and adaptable and potentially content-rich. Yet the initiative for introducing this new communications channel was graphic designers, seemingly with their ability to use an Apple Mac, not through their holistic understanding of communications. At the time of writing the lead in viral marketing appears to be taken up by web marketers and advertising. Will this be another missed opportunity by the public relations profession?

Are you ready to take up this opportunity and start managing w-o-m for your organization?

PR FUTURES DEBATE

Should w-o-m be recognized as a formal public relations discipline under the aegis of public relations professionals?

PERSONAL CHECKLIST

- Have you audited your w-o-m?
- What are your personal w-o-m brand messages?
- What are your potential w-o-m brand messages?
- Do you identify potential w-o-m messages when you communicate?

- Do you identify different w-o-m messages for different audiences?
- What free samples can you give out?
- Which targets do you need to 'seed' in future campaigns?
- What legends have you collected and circulated about you, your organization or its products and services?
- When communicating do you take into account the speed and other qualities of online communications?
- Are you guilty of thinking in slow time frames? When was the last time you took your time in writing an e-mail?
- Do you encourage everyone to send on your communications?
- Do you make sure your e-mails will not cause you embarrassment if seen by the wrong eyes?
- How often do you use net communities for information gathering, or as a sounding board for ideas?

PRELUDE TO CHAPTER 8

Each of us has a variety of networks of contacts. Not everyone is equal in your networks or other groups you seek to communicate with. By identifying key people you can create a tipping-point effect, to create a tidal wave of communications. Achieving change with limited resources and the need for any change to be sustainable makes partnership working and leveraging action through 'shadow' organizations crucial. You are probably no more than four contacts away from anyone on this planet.

8

Your networks

Each of us probably knows around 300 people on first-name terms. When you meet someone you are only a handshake away from the 300 people he or she knows on first-name terms. If the person you are introduced to then introduces you to someone else he or she knows, you are just two handshakes away from linking to a potential network of 90,000 new possible contacts.

The John Guare play (from the Stanley Milgram study, 1967) popularized the concept of 'six degrees of separation', the theory that each of us are connected to everyone else on this planet by no more than five people: that is, you know someone, who will know someone, who in turn will know someone, and so on. The six degrees of separation are not just five persons apart but are in effect five circles, or networks of acquaintances, apart.

On creativity training courses I once devised an exercise asking participants to find out how many degrees of separation there were between them and a range of well-known celebrities. Every time they were no more than three or four degrees apart. The UK television station Channel 4 devised an experiment in 2003 based on this theory. It recruited a person in Outer Mongolia, and a UK resident then had to make an interpersonal connection with this target individual. In the programme, the individual achieved the goal in eight connections. He would, however, have certainly done it in only four connections if he had worked back from the prospect.

Everyone maintains different series of networks, or what marketing guru Seth Godin (2002) calls 'hives', covering different aspects of our lives, spanning family, social and work. These networks are defined by having rules – either spoken or unspoken, standards – and a common history. They operate on a number of different and sometimes overlapping planes. Within these networks not everyone is equal or plays the same role. There is now greater understanding of the different networks governing our lives and the dynamics of them.

The outstanding public relations communicator is able to establish, nurture and maintain relevant networks, but also harness the crucial power points in them. The outstanding communicator is also likely to be a key part of other people's networks.

Each of us has personal network maps, operating on at least five different levels, consisting of:

- a personal sanctum;
- a professional sanctum, or 'professional apostles';
- an inner circle;
- an outer circle;
- membership links.

PERSONAL SANCTUM

Each of us has a personal community, a circle around us, usually of up to 15 people. You can count on these family members or friends to provide the innermost emotional core of your contacts. There is a limit to the amount of information you can handle at once; in your conscious mind you can hold between five to nine pieces of information at any one time. It is not just your information-processing abilities that are limited, but so too are your emotional capacities, where we are only capable of maintaining really close emotional relationships with between 10 and 15 people.

The well-being of your personal sanctum network acts as the bedrock for all your other networks. Maintaining a positive set of relationships with your family and friends, along with a healthy work–life balance, will provide the foundations for your wider contentment and well-being. It provides a bedrock for defining your 'realness', the real you and your inner brand, and serves as a grounding for your successful communications.

PROFESSIONAL SANCTUM

Reflect on your career and your current working life. Who has been influential in helping you move up the career ladder in whatever way, to get where you are today? Think a bit harder. Who has been really influential?

Each of us has a number of 'professional apostles', people who act as the frontline of our personal advocates. As a public relations consultant your apostle might be the person who regularly generates new business leads or referrals for you. In an organization it might be a manager who has championed your advancement. These are people who somehow stimulate things in your life and support your cause. They truly act as your advocates, by telling the world how great you are, without any prompting. Apostles believe in you wholeheartedly, and share that fact freely.

On a personal level they bring out the best in you, sometimes acting as buffers or as cushions against negative influences. They are generous with you, and you with them. You will go that extra mile, do the special favour to help them. They can afford for you to succeed without feeling threatened. These are the relationships that truly rocket you to the top.

If you want to get ahead you need to build the network of your professional sanctum to at least 15 people. At least you are helped in this quest by the fact that they are generally people predisposed to being helpful.

Anyone predisposed to be helpful is worth knowing because they:

- were brought up to be helpful to others;
- see opportunities more than others do, and view you as one;
- are secure and willing to take risks to help others;
- feel important when helping others;
- are intellectually curious;
- have a variety of networks;
- simply like you.

As part of a personal development strategy and effective personal communications campaign, regularly keep in touch with your targeted list of professional apostles. Never be more than one month away from these valuable contacts. Contact could be through sending articles on your industry, or better theirs, posting friendly memos or sending clippings. Stay current with them, no matter how busy you get. When you do so, they are reminded of you, and as you will be front of mind with them, so yours will be the number they call. A fundamental maintenance strategy of these relationships, like any networking relationship, is not to sell yourself, but rather to keep building and investing in the relationship.

Leading marketing and brand consultant Gareth Owen emphasizes the need to keep front of mind with his prospects:

You have to keep in touch, create opportunities to talk to your prospects without appearing that you are selling to them. Topical things in the trade press, appropriate gossip, even funny e-mails are all good tools to keep in touch with people.

Task: putting it into practice

Who are your apostles? Who potentially could become one of your apostles? What can you do for your apostles? What different ways can you maintain contact with your apostles?

INNER CIRCLE

You have a social capacity, a number of people that you have a genuinely social relationship with, the kind of relationship that goes with knowing who they are, and how they relate to you. Typically, the inner social group is of up to 150 people. Any larger group will start to need complicated hierarchies, rules, regulations and formal measures to try to command loyalty and social cohesion.

OUTER CIRCLE

Your outer contact could consist of anything between 300 and 1,000 acquaintances, people you are relatively comfortable with. Growth in social and geographical mobility (and also from applying the lessons of this book) will lead to an inevitable increase in the size of your outer circle. To face the challenge of managing these numbers you can profile the group, dividing them into smaller groups of contacts which can be more easily managed, prioritized and subsequently maintained.

A profiling system for a public relations consultant, for example, where it is important to develop business development contacts to provide a flow of new clients, could use a profile of:

1. **Advocates**, which might be your clients as well as professional sanctum contacts. They provide an unprompted advocacy of you, or your cause.
2. **Endorser contacts** can often be clients who could provide a prompted testimonial or advocacy for you.
3. **Awares** are people who have an awareness of you but do not use your

services or advocate you. They offer the potential to be converted into a category 1 or 2.

4. **Unawares** do not know of you, or how you might be relevant for their needs.
5. **Catch-alls** are usually contacts you might politely send a Christmas card to, but whom you do not wish to cultivate for your business or organizational development.

Competitors are often overlooked as a source of fruitful contact. Although on the surface they might be Public Enemy Number One there will still be opportunities for cooperation rather than confrontation. My experience is that I obtain between 10 and 20 per cent of my word-of-mouth referrals from 'competitors'. Often they have potential opportunities they are not in a position to capitalize on through conflict of interest, lack of resource, because it is outside their specialism, or a personal disinterest.

MEMBERSHIP

You have membership of different networks. These network hubs contain people who communicate with more people about a certain product than average. They are also known as 'opinion formers', 'influencers', 'lead users' or even 'power users'.

JUDGING THE VALUE OF THE MEMBERSHIP NETWORKS

How can you judge the relative merits of different networks? Which ones are more important and which should you be engaged with? Although the nature of hubs differs from industry to industry, the key criteria for the value of any network or hive are its relative size; centrality to its context, quality of its ability – or potential – to deliver, infrastructure and vibrancy.

Size

The overall cluster of the target network will have an impact on the scale and length of any w-o-m messages. Fads and fashions for example tend to burn up and burn out quicker in the UK and Japan than in the United States because their populations are more densely clustered. This greater proximity gives a higher level of conductivity for new ideas to be quickly assimilated, but equally causes them to mature and die at a faster rate.

The bigger the network, the more potential potency for engaging more people, generating greater awareness and stimulating further outgrowth from the core. Using Metcalfe's law, the value of a network grows as the square of the number of its users. Zipf's law revealed how the word, 'the' is used 10 times more than the tenth most popular words, which in turn are used 10 times more than the hundredth most popular words, and 1,000 times more than the thousandth. The potential for exponential growth is mind-boggling. Imagine folding a paper in half to give it twice its original thickness. How thick would the paper be if it could be folded another 40 times? It would reach from the earth to the moon!

Centrality

The centrality of a network, how important it is to your life, will be determined by its:

- **Relative importance to your needs.** If you need a network to meet your prime needs of defence or economic well-being, its status and importance to you is obviously clearly more significant than a minor interest.
- **Ability to deliver.** The true value of a network is shaped by more than its relative size: it depends on the quality and power of influence of its members in relation to the context. The most effective networks are often the 'power of the few' – small groups of active key decision makers, with short decision-making chains of individuals yielding sufficient 'power to do'. These will often wield more power than a larger network of passive individuals possessing minimal power.
- **Infrastructure.** The infrastructure of a network may range from tangible resources to the level of organization, or softer criteria of formality of membership, formal and informal powers.
- **Vibrancy.** The vibrancy is the functioning, the heartbeat of the network. It is determined by the level of commitment and frequency of participation. Key factors determining the velocity of an idea spreading include the intrinsic rewards obtained from membership, the accessibility of the group, ease of change within the group, and the promise of new discoveries and opportunities as a result of being in the group.

STRUCTURES WITHIN NETWORKS

In his book *The Tipping Point* (2002), Malcolm Gladwell describes the moment when ideas, trends and social behaviours cross a threshold, tip and spread like wildfire. In his analysis of the social dynamics underpinning changes he emphasizes the role of networks and crucially, the key players within these networks.

Using the model of how epidemics start, it is clear that the success of any kind of social epidemic is heavily dependent on the involvement of people with a particular and special set of social gifts. Gladwell identifies three kinds of people.

Connectors

Connectors know lots of people. In fact it seems they know everyone. They possess extensive inner-circle-level contacts where they know a lot of people, and make a point to communicate with them, although they do not necessarily know them in great depth.

Connectors, also known as 'alphas', are 'people specialists', and they do this as a natural part of their way of life. They are the masters of the so-called 'weak tie': that is, keeping contact with acquaintances and not just good friends. Connectors are gregarious and intensely social, and manage to occupy many different worlds, subcultures and niches. It is this last characteristic that is key to their role in spreading ideas, creating trends and opening up wider networks than intense close ties.

They have an ability to be interested in people, seeing things in them that they don't see themselves. They see the potential in you and, most importantly they see potential links for you with members of their network.

Mavens

Mavens are the 'information specialists'. The word comes from the Yiddish meaning 'one who accumulates knowledge'. They are committed to the collection of a wide range of information on a lot of different products, prices or places. Their critical role in the social epidemic is their desire to communicate their knowledge to as many others as possible. Mavens are information brokers, sharing and trading what they know. They want to help you find solutions to your problems while at the same time solving their own. Mavens are not just passive collectors of information but also tell others, and are more socially motivated than experts.

Steve Sowerby of brand consultancy Fusion Learning tells of a surprising experience when he was researching for a consumer products campaign. He discovered there are even internet chat rooms dedicated to cleaning products. By visiting the site http://groups.yahoo.com/group/wcs/ and making contact with users he was able to make access to connectors and mavens even in this market.

Salesmen (and saleswomen)

These are the 'persuaders', with the skills to persuade us even when we are unconvinced of what we are hearing. Salespeople, also known as 'bees', are masters of rapport, with a contagious and irresistible trait that makes people want to agree. They possess significant energy, enthusiasm, charm and likeability.

Godin takes the 'salesperson' concept further with his term of 'sneezer', to describe people more likely to spread new ideas, much in the same way as a sneeze spreads a germ. He also defines categories of 'promiscuous sneezers' and 'powerful sneezers'.

An exercise

Abdul, Ahmed, Akers, Anderson, Anthony, Atkins, Atkinson, Attardo, Avery, Ballard, Barber, Barlthrop, Benstock, Blackmore, Bland, Bowyer, Boyle, Bradbury, Britton, Brown, Buckingham, Buitekant, Cadbury, Carlaw, Cavanagh, Childs, Clark, Clayton, Cleary, Connolly, Cowie, Crawford, Crimmins, Crossley, Davies, Dear, Dinh, Doonan, Dunne, Dyson, Earl, Edwards, Evans, Falcus, Farrington, Ferguson, Fisher, Foster, Giles, Gilchrist, Goldstein, Goody, Gossage, Gower, Green, Gregory, Grimes, Hall, Hansen, Heed, Hillier, Hindley, Hodges, Hoffman, Holland, Holmes, Hornibrook, Hoskins, Hughes, Hurst, Hutchinson, Hutton, Illingworth, Jarvis, Jones, Kelly, Kettleborough, King, Kintish, Knight, Komaromy, Laing, Landen, Lane, Laski, Lee, Lewington, Lomas, Lowe, Lui, Lupton, McCarthy, McDermott, McNamara, Manzi, Marsh, Metcalfe, Mills, Ming, Moon, Moore, Moorwood, Morgan, Mortimer, Moss, Neville, Newman, Novara, O'Grady, O'Mahoney, Oliver, Overton, Pace, Patel, Patterson, Peters, Piggott, Preece, Pritchard, Quayle, Quinn, Ratrick, Redknapp, Reeves, Roberts, Ross, Schmidt, Singh, Sommers, Stevens, Stubbs, Tallis, Thomas, Thorogood, Timperley, Tucker, Underwood, Van Smirren, Vilas, Wainwright, Wallace, Wardell, Warren, Watson, Wiggins, Wills, Wong.

How many people do you know with a name in the list above? Give yourself a score every time you know someone (you just need to know of them in your personal network). A high score is indicative of a larger network of friends and acquaintances, a sign of more social activity creating more widespread connections.

Paul Richards is a specialist in the public sector and not-for-profit PR sectors. He is very critical of the waste in resources witnessed in many campaigns in this sector:

The people flogging cars and holidays or building global brands know what to do – spend millions on posters, TV and internet advertising, hire celebrity endorsers, create international PR stunts, sponsor polo matches and yacht races, and watch the sales rocket. For a local group or campaign, communications involves a different set of tools and tactics. Word of mouth is the most powerful form of communications in a local area – so who are the local leaders, connectors and 'radio stations'? Low-level advertising can be effective – and that might mean the newsagents' windows or the back of the prayer card in the local mosque. Getting coverage in local newspapers and tenants' newsletters might work well. Forget sponsoring the England team – sponsoring the local darts team may be just as effective.

Task: putting it into practice

Who would you identify as a connector, salesperson or maven in your networks? What potential candidates can you identify who could take these roles in your networks? Who do you know who might identify new contacts to join your networks?

THE DYNAMICS IN NETWORKS

How does communication take place in a network? One of the key studies in diffusion principles was carried out in Iowa in the 1930s (Ryan and Gross, 1943). It identified how different people play different roles in the spreading of new ideas and practices, and found that the diffusion of ideas or trends is a staged process. The first group of people to try anything new are the *innovators*, a small group around 2.5 per cent of the population. They are the more adventurous, the first to experiment and try out new things – often just because they are new.

Second are the *early adopters*, a slightly larger group of around 13.5 per cent of the population who become 'infected' by the innovators. These are the 'cool hunters', spotters of new trends and tectonic shifts in taste. They are the opinion leaders in communities, the respected, thoughtful people who watch and analyse what the innovators do and then follow suit.

The *early majority* and the *late majority* form the 'big bulge', the largest group, split into two parts, each of about 34 per cent of the population. These people are deliberately sceptical and never try anything new until others, whom they respect, try it first and show that it works.

The *laggards* are the last to take on anything new. They are the most traditional group of all, and see no reason to change. They form around 16 per cent of the population.

This provides us with a useful model for communicating a change process. It highlights the types of people we need to work with in the early stages. It also reveals that different groups will need different messages: innovators and early adopters do not share the same paradigms as the early majority and subsequent groups. Nor is there good communication between the groups. Innovators and early adopters are visionaries, seeking to be significantly different or even working for revolutionary change, prepared to be the first to try out new technologies even when they are unproven. The early majority, in contrast, need to fit change into their existing paradigms in a slow, incremental way. They occupy a paradigm where risk-taking is low or totally absent. These two different cultures are fundamentally incompatible, with a chasm between them. Communications do not just slide smoothly between them.

It is essential that any communications to the early majority are delivered in a way that they are able to work with and take on board. This is where the connectors, mavens and salespeople can play a crucial role in the communications process. They take ideas and information from highly specialized worlds and translate them into languages other groups can understand.

This process can involve dropping some of the detail and focusing at greater depth on some key features of the message. The information is presented in such a way as to lessen any sense of dissonance among the target audience, and inflate the scale of any benefits involved in a change to outweigh any initially perceived disadvantages. If you communicate through, and focus resources on, the connectors, mavens and salespeople, the early majority come on board and enable a change process to 'tip' and effective communications to get underway.

Task: putting it into practice

Reflect on a recent campaign. Could you have targeted different groups such as innovators and early adopters? How guilty were you of using just one message to different adopter groups?

SHADOW ORGANIZATIONS

Most organizations, to use management consultancy jargon, are nonlinear feedback networks; they possess a multitude of criss-crossing relationships, lines of communication, which are receptive to any communication. It is these features of nonlinearity with their spontaneous relations between people, irregular sharing of information and informal learning processes that make organizational networks a dynamic force which can readily adjust to change and innovation.

These informal networks can act as 'shadow organizations', creatively interpreting and modifying official strategies, and are the real drivers for innovation and change. It is the shadow organization, the one that is not reflected in the organization chart, that often actually makes the system work despite the constraints of the formal body it operates within. Usually much informal shadow activity gets picked up by the formal institution, and after a time becomes institutionalized, making the organization official.

Shadow organizations can be better than formal organizations at incorporating learning and experience, and are less prescriptive, so making them suitable for creating temporary platforms of interest. These networks do however require a lot of energy to maintain their vibrancy, and it can be difficult motivating people where there is little formal control or face-to-face contact.

Helen Kettleborough of Pace microtechnology emphasizes the importance of maintaining a broad range of contacts:

> Often the people with the answers, the pointers to help you get where you want to go, may not formally be the people with the most obvious job titles. Keeping in with a broad range of contacts – even if it's just bumping into people in the canteen or on the stairs – is vital in keeping your finger on the pulse or making things happen.

An example of overlooking the value of informal contacts is the mistake made by many conference organizers who try to cram too much in their programme schedules. Delegates consequently have tight schedules with little scope for interaction with other conference goers, or other potential contacts. Anyone who has been away on an official team-building event will recognize that often the most valuable contacts and learning come through the informal elements – the time at the bar, or just queuing at the buffet.

Barry Sheerman, a Member of Parliament in the UK, explained how he valued the division system in the House where everyone queues to register their vote: 'It provides an opportunity to collar ministers in the queue, when it could take weeks to arrange a formal appointment.'

Outstanding communicators build into their daily schedules opportunities for connecting with potential shadow networks, and capitalize on the opportunities they create from these contacts.

SOURCES OF INTELLIGENCE

Networking contacts can also provide valuable marketing intelligence. Gerry Carson, former director of corporate affairs for the Royal Hospitals in Belfast, recalls how he had a difficult job to position his organization as politically neutral while serving an extremely politically divided community. His networking contacts were invaluable in knowing who was behind what might appear on the surface as an innocuous sponsorship request, especially when in reality there was a poisoned chalice behind it.

Research into the links between universities and biotechnology companies in the United States has consistently found that a high proportion of collaborations come about through personal connections – not through policy instruments, funding conditions or institutional arrangements. In one study, performed in the late 1980s, a high proportion of technology-transfer events were based on contacts that had been formed by researchers years before, when they were graduate students.

This observation points to the dynamic and interactive culture of the US research system, where it is not uncommon to receive an undergraduate degree at one institution, a PhD at another, and do postdoctoral research at a third before taking up a faculty position at a fourth, where each jump might take the individual to a different part of the country. As a result research establishments in the United States are vastly interconnected and networked through personal contacts, creating extensive links between regions and organizations, as well as within them. This situation contrasts with their counterparts in Europe, which features specialization by region and institution. Consequently this appears to hamper an equivalent mobility – and the collaboration that goes with it. ('The business', *FT* weekend magazine, 22 June 2002).

NETWORK AUDITS

A number of simple tools can be used to map out your networking requirements, your current position and where you have network gaps. Using a networking matrix you can identify your target audiences and groups, people with the ability to say 'Yes' or 'No' to impact on your future success. Using these targets as one axis of your matrix, you can then identify your existing lead networkers. Using a criterion based on the quality of the relationship, you can identify your points of contact, and more importantly where you have inadequate contacts, to enable you to take remedial action.

This is a possible set of measures on a criterion for measuring the degree of contact:

A = decision maker;
B = can influence decision maker;
C = knows decision makers but no direct influence;
D = recognizable peer of decision makers;
E = no contact/connection.

THE POWER OF PARTNERSHIPS

We live in an age where more is wanted with less, whether it is resource, time or contacts, yet we all have finite resources. One strategy to overcome this paradox is to develop partnerships, win–win relationships with others who can work with you to accomplish joint goals by pooling resources.

One of the key skills of outstanding communicators is their ability to identify potential partners, and work with them to achieve their common goals. Partnerships provide:

- greater combined resources;
- wider legitimacy to your mission, implying that if other people are involved then it must have greater validity;
- endorsement as a sign of approval;
- reduction in barriers between collaborators;
- greater connectivity, offering additional communications channels between the partners;
- a larger pool of experience and knowledge to call on;
- access to each partner's individual networks;
- additional synergies from joint working;
- longer-term sustainability to the outcomes of the partnership.

Yet the concept of partnership sometimes receives a jaundiced reaction, particularly in the regeneration sector, where the word is often glibly used as a magic wand-like solution to major challenges. Partnership is like marriage: just as there are good and bad marriages some partnerships are fine, but others can be abusive and unhealthy.

In the context of a fast-moving era individuals and organizations face a real challenge in trying to keep pace with exponential fast-moving environments. Collaborative working relationships can help you keep pace with developments. The growth in collaboration also has benefits in helping you or your organization define more clearly what you are, and why you do what you do: you do not have to be all things to all people. Equally, with an effective network of partners you can adapt and flexibly respond to any new opportunities so you are not restricting yourself too greatly.

In your partnerships you will need to call up different networks as and when you need them. Networks are only as strong as the capabilities of the individuals who make them up. The dominant organizations of the future might be not stable, permanent corporations but rather elastic networks that sometimes exist for no more than a day or two to meet a specific need.

Ingredients for successful partnership working are very much based on a win–win philosophy. Both sides need to:

● have sufficient shared values between them, particularly sharing the key values for their project;
● respect the right of the others to be present and have a valid role to play in the future relationship;
● recognize and respect the differences between the partners;
● understand the restraints faced by other partners, in terms of resources, decision-making power, and values;
● appreciate that although successful partnership working will speed up aspects of getting access to key decision makers and improve service delivery, the inherent need to engage other parties inevitably might lead to longer decision-making timescales, particularly in the early days of the partnership;
● continually negotiate and renegotiate mutual expectations, commitments and actions to keep the relationship vibrant and alive;
● maintain trust and belief in the partnership: trust is the essential lubricant of partnership working.

When choosing partners, factors to consider are:

● the strength of their relationship with the target market;
● the value of their brand;
● the degree of connectivity with the target market;
● personal commitment of key personnel in the partner team to the partnership;
● recognition of win–win solutions and philosophy along with sufficient shared values to make the relationship work;
● a track record of partnership delivery in the target market;
● whether potential partners might have a hidden agenda, and could potentially use the partnership merely as a foil to achieve other ends.

Barry Sheerman MP is one of the longest serving members of Parliament and the chair of the Parliamentary Committee on Education and Employment. He is a passionate supporter of social enterprises:

Achieving social change you need to bring together interesting, entrepreneur-minded people in the private and public sectors and create new networks. Tidal waves of change are possible with the right vision, connections and positive attitude to working together. Partnership is fundamental to creating successful change in our society.

The partnership concept does not just rest within a group of communicators, but can also be used to engage the audience. Lead or 'beta' customers, your innovators or early adopters, can be engaged in the relationship to provide feedback on specific issues. Charles Leadbeater (2000) observes that in modern knowledge-driven economies, consuming will become more of a relationship than an act. The more knowledge-intensive products become, the more consumers will have to be involved in completing their production, tailoring the product to their needs. Consumption of knowledge-intensive products is not just joint and shared, but is additive as well: consumers can add to the product's qualities.

OUTSTANDING PUBLIC RELATIONS COMMUNICATORS BUILD AND USE THEIR NETWORKS

Look at the rise to greatness of any outstanding public relations communicator. He or she will invariably have created a series of networks which he or she has used to gain leverage in activities to promote the individual or his or her organization. The Chartered Institute of Public Relations in the UK represents a major network channel for practitioners to help advance their careers and interests.

Outstanding communicators do not just rely on their own personal qualities, or skilfully create and distribute messages, but achieve real success by building, using and maintaining effective networks.

Task: putting it into practice

What partnerships could you establish at an individual or organization level to advance your mutual interests? What can you do for your partners?

PR FUTURES DEBATE

Should public relations managers be in charge of managing their organization's network maps? Who is in charge of identifying the key contacts for the future success of the organization? Should mass-media campaigns only be contemplated after any network campaigns targeted at the few are exhausted?

PERSONAL CHECKLIST

- Who is in your own professional sanctum of contacts?
- Have you identified your different networks of contacts and profiled them in any way by their roles as connectors, salespeople or mavens?
- What do you do to manage the different network contacts you have?
- How much do you tailor your messages to meet the varying needs of different groups when you launch a new product or service?

PRELUDE TO CHAPTER 9

Networking is not just about who you know, but who the people you are networking with know. It is often a stepping-stone process rather than a direct hit to reaching your target.

No one is as smart as everyone. Successful networking is not about selling but is based on a philosophy of achieving mutual win–win goals. Networking can be targeted and managed to leverage greater results. Anyone within 12 feet of you provides a networking opportunity. Your business card is your personal brand statement. Networking can be anything from attending business events to running a public relations football team.

9

Managing your networking

I once met a woman at a business event who told me about her research project on millionaire entrepreneurs (I assumed she had chosen that subject for academic reasons). She asked me if I was a millionaire. I mused out loud that I was in many ways, but not in money terms. The woman seemed to lose any interest in extending the conversation, and in a rather curt manner moved off.

Had she continued the conversation I could have told her although I am not a millionaire myself, I do personally know, and could successfully have introduced her to, at least six millionaires. I would have been quite happy to help, believing it would be of interest to the millionaires and pander to their egos. It would have also helped this stranger, who was seemingly doing interesting things.

Networking is not just about who you know, but who the people you are networking with know. It is often a stepping-stone process rather than a direct hit to reach your target.

No one is as smart as everyone. Connecting with other people offers you the potential to tap into their knowledge, experience, world-view and connections. Public relations people are natural networkers; in many instances they do not possess direct-line authority over other colleagues whose cooperation they require to achieve a goal. Public relations people tend to have values of sharing information, achieving mutual goals, seeing the bigger picture, and working with different stakeholder communities.

WHAT EXACTLY IS NETWORKING?

Networking is not just about taking. It is fundamentally about giving. It involves a profound philosophical approach of being interested in other people and earnestly wishing to help them. In networking you get what you give. The way to reap fruit from any networking activity is to ask what you can do to help this other person through your own resources as well as your networks and connections.

As an equation networking can be defined as:

networking = personal public relations + cross-fertilization of contacts × doing something to add value to the other person's life

Networking is a discipline which needs to be managed. It is a marketing discipline and tool where the public relations professional should be in charge. (It is also a skill for use in every aspect of your life.)

Imagine the career paths of two different people. One is very good at her job, puts in a full day at the office, but barely leaves her desk. She stays with the same firm all her life. The other is perhaps technically not as good at her job, but in contrast she gets out and about in her work and her wider life. She goes to meetings. She connects very readily with anyone she meets. She makes herself known. Anyone who meets her invariably walks away with her business card. Which of the two is more likely to get on and be successful in her career?

By making connections you are opening up new points of engagement with others and their networks. You are bringing yourself front of mind when they wonder who might be able to help with any problem they face. You are using face-to-face communications, the most powerful communications tool for establishing trust and reputation. You can open doors to new opportunities through making the right connections, like the old adage, 'It's not what you know but who you know.'

Too many people ostensibly in public relations, work in, rather than on, their business. They need to consider what their networks consist of and how they should use them to tell the world what is different about their work, and how it is better than any of its competitors. So why is networking in many ways the Cinderella of marketing communications? A cynic might observe that 'networking' is very close to 'not-working'. The lounge lizard syndrome might come to mind, someone seemingly wasting away time in a series of 'jollies', enjoying the pleasures of social activities without a focus on achieving real business and communications goals.

A networking approach might also encourage over-elaboration of the communications process. Rather than just directly go to a target you might miss a vital opportunity by taking too long trying to identify a mutual connection, or by choosing the wrong acquaintance, someone with little status or relevance to your challenge.

The status of networking in public relations has also suffered from a backlash against the image of the early days of practice, where influencing key contacts with a gin and tonic was seen as stereotypical. As motor industry public relations specialist Heather Yaxley muses, 'There's a good reason why PR practitioners should be proud schmoozers – it's essential to know the right people to target with appropriate messages and how to get things done quickly and effectively.'

Networking is also seen as something operating at an intuitive level that somehow happens to those who seem to be 'natural networkers'. This logic implies that good networking is something just done by good networkers, with no recognition of the processes and skills underpinning the discipline of networking.

The fundamental challenge you face as a networker is that no matter how proficient and organized you are at managing the process and organization of networking, it is no good if you know 500 very powerful and influential people yet every one of them thinks you are an idiot. Your inner brand and the way you communicate must be credible for other people to want to entertain a dialogue or connection with you. Will Kintish runs a specialist consultancy in networking and presentation skills. (He was recommended to the author by our mutual friend Steve McDermott.) Will identifies self-belief as the cornerstone of networking skills:

> Most people think that networking is something you are born with. But I have trained and equipped several thousand delegates with the skills to be effective networkers. The fundamental starting point is you have got to believe you can help others through your connections and what you can do in your work. If you don't believe you can help others you shouldn't be in business.

Task: putting it into practice

When did you last network? What opportunities are there for you to network more over the next week? What can you do to encourage your colleagues to network more?

SOME MYTHS ABOUT NETWORKING

The heart of good public relations business has been that if you do a good job or deliver a good product for a client, he or she will come back to you. Yet in a fast-moving world your delighted customer might in the interim build new relationships with a rival. No matter how wonderful your service, you need to maintain visibility and contact in your relationships in order to stay front of mind of your contacts.

There is also a cherished view that if you do a good job for someone he or she will tell others about it. Your service however needs to be highly distinctive, even legendary, for it to create memorable word-of-mouth (w-o-m) by itself.

Much service activity is underpinned by the hope that if you give blindly to others you can expect people to respond positively. This principle is fundamental to networking: building equity – a bank of goodwill – will provide dividends for the future. Such philanthropy can however take time for any 'payback' to come through. You therefore need to structure your activities to deliver quick, as well as long-term, wins.

Another myth about networking is that it takes up too much time, yet as part of a managed communications strategy effective networking will actually save you time. It can help you cut corners by getting through to your targets faster, cutting down on decision-making time, getting through to the real decision maker quicker, or creating greater trust in your partner relationships.

Networking is sometimes mistakenly confused with selling, and seen as prostituting personal contacts for commercial gain. The fundamental is that networking is actually a giving process, more often gathering information rather than deals. Rather than prostituting contacts it is about providing true value to all those you are linking together.

There is also a view that you cannot have your cake and eat it. That's wrong. With intensive time pressures creating greater unity between our working and wider lives, regarding the people you connect with as your friends will create win–win opportunities.

Some people regard networking as belonging to 'people who have connections'. Yet unless they are royalty, most successful communicators have had to create their networks of contacts through their own efforts. Every networker has had to begin somewhere.

Task: putting it into practice

In what different ways can you help the people you meet? What services, tacit knowledge, contacts or opportunities could you offer them? How can you make their world better?

STRATEGIES FOR NETWORKING

The starting point for effective networking is to establish a strategy identifying what you are seeking from the process. Andy Gilbert of personal development consultancy Go MAD uses the following check questions to establish a map for his networking activities and provide the strategy for involving others in his activities:

- Who do you want to get involved in your assignment?
- What do you want to achieve from their involvement?
- How can you get their buy-in to your world?
- What other ways can you connect with them?
- What barriers are there to achieving the above?
- What ways are there to overcome these barriers?
- What are the risks and implications for them in getting involved with you?
- What resources do you have directly and indirectly to involve other people?
- Who could you involve to get them involved?
- What dead people could you use in your quest? (Before you rush off to a ouija board, this technique is essentially asking what information, or inspiration about the challenge you face, you can gain from dead people's biographies.)
- What self-limiting beliefs or assumptions are holding you back?

Using these checklist questions you can create a networking map for your campaign, as well as create objectives and identify the crucial elements of any strategy: your starting-point, where you want to go and what is the line of least resistance to get you to your goals.

THE MORE EXACTLY YOU DEFINE YOUR POTENTIAL TARGETS THE EASIER IT WILL BE TO FIND THEM

Defining the people who are likely to be your best prospects will ultimately save wasted time and effort. You need to define your business or goals, and also define your perfect prospect. Great networking contacts are those who act as 'bridges' to your ultimate target. These people work in one part of your target organization and can introduce you to other people in different vertical business units within their networks. Include longer-term strategies in your plans. If getting through to the key decision makers in your sector is a problem, identify the rising stars and pin your colours and support to their cause.

Not having the time is not a valid excuse for not networking. Combine different interests to create win–win opportunities. In my younger days I was a keen footballer, and I came up with the idea of establishing a PR football team which played against teams of journalists. We had a lot of fun, I got to know some great people and media contacts through the team, and my one and only goal, a 20-yard volley, still sparkles in my mind!

CHARACTERISTICS OF OUTSTANDING NETWORKERS

Master networkers keep their eyes open and maintain a positive attitude to bringing people together. They use active listening to learn about others' needs, and use their information and contacts to genuinely strive to help others.

Networkers are able to get leverage off their personal visibility. You need to ask yourself if your profile is sufficiently high. Do you know your counterparts in other parts of the business, or in competitor organizations? Do you get involved with other bodies, go to exhibitions, attend 'big picture' events, publicize yourself, comment regularly and work to be seen as an expert?

Outstanding networkers also publicize their wants. At the time of writing I am searching for a business partner to make a range of furniture for creative businesses, using a new concept I have devised, which I call 'warm desking'. I have already protected my core interests by registering a company name and relevant domain names. Now I mention my quest to find a suitable partner for this venture in networking encounters. Using this approach is harnessing the lowest-cost advertising channel available to you.

Far Eastern cultures have long recognized the value of personal networks, practising what they call 'Guanxi'. Western communications practice has belatedly recognized the significance of this dimension in formalizing its 'know-who' skills. Unlike 'know-how' individuals who preserve their own knowledge and information and tend to be inward looking, 'know-who' individuals are marked by their skills in building relationships to extend their own know-how and enhance their own ability to communicate. The best strategy is to piggyback or harness different people with relevant knowledge for your needs. Know-who individuals excel at connectivity to build the right connections with the right people. Knowledgeable people know facts. Successful networkers know people.

Although great networkers come in all shapes and sizes, marketing guru John Timperley characterizes two different styles of networking, with contrasting extrovert and introvert personalities. The extrovert connector is characterized by:

- having many contacts;
- enjoying making new contacts and being socially confident;
- preferring talking to writing (and listening!);
- being primarily interested in people;
- brainstorming and easily sparking off ideas with others;
- leading in building relationships;
- wanting to be the centre of attention.

Introvert connectors:

- are more comfortable operating with their existing contacts;
- are slower in taking the initiative socially;
- prefer writing (and listening) to talking;
- have a few very good contacts, rather than lots of low-intensity, super-ficial relationships;
- prefer to see how a relationship develops before getting deeply involved;
- want to be in the audience rather than centre stage;
- are more comfortable with getting ideas alone.

There is no excuse for not being a networker. Just use the style which suits you. Recognize your strengths and play them to the full. Compensate for any weaknesses by working with colleagues and contacts. That is what networking is all about.

Alan Preece of the University of East Anglia explains about his networking style:

I would not consider myself an extrovert networker. I do however make every effort to build around me a network of extrovert connectors. They are great fun to be around and I can tap into and harness their networks to help me achieve my goals. Hopefully I add some value back by becoming part of their network.

MAKING THE CONTACT: HOW TO WORK THE ROOM

Anyone within 12 feet of you is someone you can network with. Any opportunity can be a networking one. Dropping your children off at school you might get talking to other parents and carers. I bumped into my local MP at the supermarket. On these occasions, the challenge is to be alert and respond to the opportunity, although you should take care not to compromise an otherwise social situation. Often the way to capitalize on the connection is to exchange social chat and then identify a good time when it is convenient to get in touch to progress any possible business matters.

There will be times when you face formal events and meetings. Good networkers know how to capitalize on any opportunity. They are able to work a room, make new connections and bring different people together.

Many people are weighed down by a fear of rejection, yet people expect to be approached by strangers in business situations. Conversations can be short without being superficial. It is possible to have a good in-depth conversation in under 10 minutes.

Overselling is a sin. No one likes being sold at, especially in an unsolicited context. It is bad networking form and also bad sales strategy. People buy trust first before they buy products.

Outstanding networkers research events, identifying who will be there and who they want to see, rather than just pressing the flesh with everyone they meet. Asking the host who is coming, or examining any guest or delegate list, will help you identify potential prospects. At an event, asking people you meet 'Do you know anyone here?' can be useful in identifying movers and shakers, or at the very least getting potted histories of other guests. You can even ask people to introduce you to potential targets, as long as there is a credible reason for doing so: 'I hope you won't mind introducing me to ... as I'm interested in ...'.

BREAKING THE ICE

A journalist attended an event that Her Royal Highness Princess Anne was present at. She had been introduced to and had spoken with a line of people. He decided to find out what the princess actually said to them. Each replied, 'She asked, "Did you come here by train?"' If it is good enough for royalty then it can be good enough for everyone else. Opening lines do not need to be the secret formula of rocket science. The important thing is to get the conversation going.

Openers can be low-key personal questions such as:

- Referential: 'Who do you know here?'
- Shared experience: 'How did you get here?'
- Shared expectation: 'What will be the most interesting parts of the seminar?'
- Shared need: 'What's the food like here?'

The questions must be open ones, which cannot be answered by just a 'yes' or a 'no'. They must also be easily answerable, and offer potential to build commonality between you and this new person you are seeking to get to know better.

Avoid obscure or jarring questions. The opening question is your foot in the door to enable you to move the relationship on smoothly. The best questions are ones that suggest a genuine interest in the other person: 'How did you get the break into your business?', 'What advice would you give for someone just starting?' or 'How are you different from your competition?'

EXCHANGE OF CONTACT INFORMATION

Try to use the person's name as soon as possible. A person's name, according to Dale Carnegie, is 'the sweetest sound anyone ever hears'. The next stage could be to ensure you exchange business cards. How do you get other people to accept your card and avoid the impression of thrusting your card upon them? The easiest way is to ask for theirs. I discovered this technique quite by accident. I once met a chartered building surveyor on a health and safety training course for small businesses. At the time I was about to buy a property, so I needed the services of a property valuer. I asked the surveyor if he knew anyone who could help, and handed over my business card. The surveyor spotted the reference to public relations, and asked, 'Do you do brochures?' This led to a discussion on his needs, which eventually generated work for my consultancy in a rebranding project. We subsequently became firm friends. I eventually returned the compliment by using the surveyor to project manage the building of a new media centre.

There is a lot to be said for Far Eastern traditions in exchanging cards. In these countries the card is given and received with both hands, and the recipient scrutinizes its contents carefully for some time to avoid giving offence to the giver. Reading the card helps you fix key details. Try to say the new contact's name aloud in your head. As a memory tool, picture someone with the same name to help store and register the name. Also, repeat his or her name when speaking to him or her.

In the early stages of the conversation do not give too much detail about yourself. Avoid bragging or appearing as if you are trying to score points. Your initial questions should be earnest and avoid coming across as an interrogation. (Your tone of voice is important here.) Do not seek free advice or come across with the hard sell. If you feel you have some relevant advice to offer, always ask the person if it is all right for you to make a suggestion that you believe will help him or her.

When asked what you do, do not reply with your job title or function, such as 'I work in public relations.' Instead highlight your service – the benefits you offer your customers, or what is special about you – and make it relevant to the person you are talking to. Be clear and concise, remembering the 'seven-second syndrome': people's impression of you is fixed in the first seven seconds, so what you say needs to be distinctive, relatable and engaging.

I run three different businesses, so I use three different forms of introduction, depending on which is most relevant to my new contact:

- As a public relations consultant, I say, 'Hello, I'm Andy Green. I get my clients the reputation they deserve.'
- As a creativity trainer and facilitator, I say, 'Hello, I'm Andy Green. I stretch people's thinking to enable them to achieve more.'
- As a director of a media and creativity centre I say, 'Hello, I'm Andy Green. I run one of the country's most creative workplaces, which is Britain's only moo-ing building.'
- For situations where I need to combine all three roles, I say, 'Hello I'm Andy Green. I get people to think differently, so they can achieve more with less.'

Task: putting it into practice

How do you introduce yourself? What ways can this be improved? Check how your colleagues introduce themselves.

YOUR POWERFUL FRIEND, YOUR BUSINESS CARD

The first tool of the effective networker is the business card. In addition to containing your core contact details, your business card should also be seen as a branding device to visually (and tactilely) convey your image. Your card can also carry your positioning, and even act as a mini icon. (Many people remember my creativity consultancy business card because it has a hole in the middle of it – an idea inspired by my daughter Lizzie when she was 13.) Always carry cards with you. Always have emergency supplies easily at hand.

RAPPORT: THERE'S LIKENESS AT THE END OF THE TUNNEL

In the film *Groundhog Day*, Bill Murray plays a lecherous television presenter in pursuit of his female colleague. Bill is trapped in a time-locked world where he gets to live through the same day again and again. Each day brings an advance in his pursuit of his object of lust, as he learns different things about her, her likes and dislikes, turn-ons and turn-offs, until ultimately he gets to the point of succeeding in turning around the relationship from enmity to love. None of us have the opportunity presented by a Groundhog Day, yet it is possible to establish some common rapport in our encounters, to enable us to engage effectively and achieve common goals with other people.

Rapport comes at the times when you seem to instantly 'hit it off' with someone, where there is mutual respect, trust and sincerity, along with shared experiences and common interests. Just as you can build rapport, it is also possible to lose it, by indicating a lack of interest or failing to deliver.

Rapport is created through a process. You go through:

- **Acknowledgement.** You can probably recall times when you were introduced to someone and he or she failed verbally, or particularly non-verbally, to take an interest in you and offer respect.
- **Understanding based on initial impressions.** Is this person a PLU (person like us), or is there some other commonality? Be very wary of forming and making the wrong assessment from initial impressions.
- **Acceptance.** This is an agreement explicitly or implicitly to continue the dialogue, and carry on the relationship.
- **Respect** comes with an emerging emotional dimension to the relationship.

- **Trust** is created when you increase the level of commitment to each other. Each of you feels confident the other will deliver, and deal with any concerns openly and in a genuine desire for accord. There is the belief that each will act in the other's best interests.
- **Bonding** emerges as a sense of real affinity, whether it is based on professional respect, friendship, love, or support to create a difficult-to-break relationship.

Here are some tips for creating rapport:

- **Smile** – although you should be careful of appearing insincere. The imperative is to create a special smile for each unique person in front of you.
- **Make the other person feel special.** Paul Carroll, the former managing director of Communique public relations, first came up to me at an industry event in Manchester and said, 'You're Andy Green. I've wanted to meet you for ages.' It turned out Paul is a supporter of Leeds United (a deadly rival of my own team), but I could not fail to be won over instantly. Showing interest in other people is paramount. Respond and engage fully with their dialogue. One of the problems of using formal presentation materials such as PowerPoint is that it tends to force you to stick to your script rather than going with the flow and fully immersing in and nurturing the live dialogue.
- **Be interested in the other person.** This is more important than your being interesting to him or her. Even the most evidently successful of people will always be engaged if you show genuine curiosity about them. If you are talking to someone at the top of their fame ask how he or she got started. Better still, ask him or her for advice: 'If I want to be as successful as you, what should I be doing now?' No celebrity I have ever dealt with has ignored this approach.
- **Match, mirror and maintain your physical stance with the person you are with.** You can establish a physical rapport by harmonizing your position, posture, stance, gestures, language and even breathing. This should be done with subtlety and inconspicuously. Poor rapport also can be generated by the physical situation: for example, if the other person is behind a large desk and you are not. The tools of rapport are very powerful, so powerful that you can even attend 'How to flirt' training courses, which evidently teach you to create rapport.

  If someone's non-verbal messages suggest a negative or ill-at-ease mental state, such as arms tightly folded, carefully adopt the same position. Match the pose for a brief period then come out of it, and the other person will often follow suit.

  Sometimes you will need to break a rapport, such as when you want to finish a phone conversation without appearing brusque. The answer is simply to stand up. This move unconsciously communicates itself and acts as a trigger to prompt the other person to conclude the conversation.

The matching should also extend to your clothing.

- **Empathize and establish commonality.** Always try to see the world from the other person's viewpoint. Understand what motivates him or her, how his or her perspective is different from yours. Respect his or her right to be different.

- **Listen and look to spot cues that could identify common interests or views.** We feel closer to people who have something in common with us. It makes people feel safe and lessens potential dissonance about the fear of the unknown.

  People tend to like and associate with those similar to them, in what is called 'homophily'. They respond to cues such as people being like-minded, and of similar age, education, income, beliefs, politics, religion, physical characteristics, height and so on.

Task: putting it into practice

Think back to any negotiation or meeting where there was conflict initially. How well did you build or create rapport to help the subsequent communication? Think back to recent conversations. How well did other people create rapport with you?

FOLLOW THROUGH

Even if you are outward-focused, attending lots of events and making lots of potential connections, the effectiveness of your networking can still be limited. Imagine someone listening to a radio who keeps rapidly moving from one station to another in the hope of catching a song he likes. The reality of this experience is that he might occasionally catch a favourite tune, yet his listening experience will be marred by superficiality: much activity with little end result to really show for his efforts. A lot of public relations communicators' networking resembles this experience. Unless you follow through effectively, your networking will be fruitless. Research on selling shows that a buyer usually needs seven quality contacts before he or she decides to buy.

Let's say you have been to a really good event, made contact with a number of high-quality potential contacts, and successfully swapped cards. What do you need to do next? First, make sure you capture live information from your encounters. It is very easy to forget key details you have learnt about the person, and also the context of where you met. A tip to overcome this is to write on the back of the person's card as soon as possible any key details or message, and the date of meeting. (Note that this is socially acceptable in the UK but might not be so in other parts of the world.)

Acknowledge the contact, by phone if there was a specific request to do so, or there is something urgent and important you need to tell the person. Usually you should write. A letter has the advantage of showing personal interest. An e-mail provides an easy response device and enables the recipient to capture your contact details on his or her system.

If you make a promise to your contact, make sure you deliver on it. If you promise to get in touch, get in touch.

Is there anything you could do for the person? There could be useful contacts you could make available to him or her, shared relevant experience, or even a personal memento.

Once you have established your new relationship you need to maintain it. Keep in touch on a regular basis by sending articles, press cuttings or e-newsletters. Invite the person to events. If something interests you, would it similarly be of interest to him or her? Consider arranging social or professional activities to create opportunities to build the relationship, from acknowledgement to bonding.

Being an active communicator you will invariably have a hectic schedule. You will face problems of encountering people at networking events who want you to discuss something which you might feel is of low priority. One tip is to ask the person to contact you on a certain date in the near future. If he or she is committed and genuinely interested, he or she will make the call. Putting the onus on other people forces them to indicate whether or not they are serious, committed and organized.

KEEP A SYSTEM

You need to maintain a system for keeping track of your contacts. This might use a basic card file or a sophisticated software program such as Access or Goldmine. The system needs to keep all the contact details, with additional information such as where you met each person, how you know him or her and other relevant personal details. Log subsequent contacts. Ideally your system should be able to record birthdays, and be cross-referenced with a diary to remind you when to contact each individual.

MAINTAIN DISCIPLINE

Networking requires discipline. You need to invest time in creating and maintaining relationships. You might have the most fantastic interpersonal skills; however if you do not keep up contact you will be forgotten, or certainly not front of mind when potential opportunities arise.

The need to maintain the values of your personal brand is crucial to effective networking, as John Timperley observes:

> Large companies usually have sophisticated contact programmes for their 'alumni' – people who used to be employed by them who have now gone to work elsewhere. They will often provide new work opportunities in their new roles. It is often ironic how following up these alumni can actually be unproductive, and even counter-productive. When presenting for new work these alumni contacts find they have not maintained effective relationships with them and instead of being 'warm' to their former employers, they are now extremely cold. They believe (possibly rightly) that the contact has been renewed only because there's a sniff of new business in the air. Nobody likes feeling they are used. The moral is to keep your contacts going and maintain a genuine relationship based on integrity and respect.

The problem with managing your networking is that it can often be an important but not urgent item in your work schedule; no one is going to get on the phone to complain you are not networking.

BUYING IN NETWORKERS

An outstanding example of an organisation that capitalized on buying in networking contacts is stadium seating manufacturer Pel plc. It capitalized on the opportunities presented by the move from standing to all-seating stadia in the UK following the Hillsborough disaster, by appointing Ted Croker, the former Football Association secretary, as company chair.

An associate of the company describes the benefits this brought to the business:

> Ted was extremely well known, not only to football clubs but also to FIFA, UEFA [the governing bodies for international football] and everything else …. Because he never had allegiance to any particular club he was seen as a fair-minded person, so it was certainly very handy to have him as figurehead of the company …. It expanded by word of mouth. These football clubs all talk to each other. One of the things chairmen will ask each other is, 'Do you know who does this, who does that, and who did your seating?' Someone would recommend Pel and say, 'Oh, you won't have any problems with them, they're market leaders and good guys, I'd recommend them.'

Another colleague recalls how 'We were very successful in Ted introducing us to various clubs. What we set out was for Ted to endorse us. With his credibility it immediately got the confidence of the chairman or stadium manager' (BBC, 2003).

Buying in an expert source can provide instant access to his or her networks and the halo effect of his or her personal brand.

Task: putting it into practice

Who can help you be more successful in your career? Who can you help to be more successful in their careers?

IS NETWORKING A FORMAL MARKETING COMMUNICATIONS TOOL?

Networking is the Cinderella of marketing communications. It rarely gets a mention in marketing communications texts. In contrast there are a large number of personal development books, seminars and specialist consultancies on 'how to network'. Networking will increase in significance as people realize its potential to achieve more with less and create win–win opportunities. Its status as a discipline will increase and it will be used with even greater sophistication.

The direct marketing industry has sought to capture customer relationship management (CRM) as a process and activity under its auspice. The hype for CRM, and the subsequent experiences when expensive software systems failed to deliver, highlighted how it is difficult to impose a relationship from without. CRM was based on a false premise of a relationship focused on exploitation rather than win–win. It is all very well for an organization to have a vast data bank on customer preferences and choices, but this is ultimately undermined if customers call in and face a baffling telephone response system.

The future must be built around relationship management systems built from within, starting from existing relationships and building networks with other stakeholders. The public relations profession has a great opportunity to be master of the various strategies and tactics of networking, to use both for its own benefit, and also as a communications tool in any campaign.

PR FUTURES DEBATE

Are you ready to take up the opportunity and start managing networking for your organization?

PERSONAL CHECKLIST

- Who do you know who could provide useful contacts for you?
- Who do you want to reach, and working back from his or her position, do you know any mutual acquaintances who could act as intermediaries?
- In what ways can you help your networking contacts?
- How can you be more effective at building rapport with your contacts?
- Do you follow up contacts you make?
- Do you keep in touch with contacts?
- Do you maintain your personal networking database?
- Do you have a hobby, personal interest or activity that you could turn into the basis for a networking opportunity?

PRELUDE TO CHAPTER 10

The context in which you present information determines its value and significance. The successful communicator seeks win–win solutions and gets targets to make 'half-step' moves to change their behaviour. Even sharing a birthday with someone odious can make you change your attitude to that person.

10

The power of context – managing the environment for your communications

I once made the mistake of sitting in the front row at a show by comedian Ken Dodd, whose act featured him picking on different members of the audience. 'You sir, what is your surname?' he asked. I told him it was 'Green', and he said, 'Do you know that means handsome, generous and kind?' I preened myself. He then asked what my first name was. 'Andy' he concluded, means 'not very.'

No matter how well crafted or superbly presented your message, its communications value is defined by its context. The spread of information and ideas is dependent on the conditions and circumstances of the times and places in which they occur. The success of your communications is also determined by how far you need to move people from their existing perceptions and mind-states: the longer the journey you need them to take, the more difficult will be your challenge.

Abraham Lincoln's Gettysburg address and Winston Churchill's wartime radio broadcasts are considered outstanding examples of communication. Yet would they be so revered, respected and recognized had the Southern States of America or Nazi Germany won their respective wars?

If Shakespeare had been Dutch or Spanish, would he have been so famous? Regardless of his innate talents his success was helped by a number of key external factors: the English language had just emerged as a tongue coherent to the modern ear; Britain was beginning to establish itself as a major imperial power, usurping The Netherlands, its then near-rival, and creating a global market for English language products; the English language possessed an inherent flexibility, providing a greater raw resource and more ability to show subtlety and inventiveness than, say, could be achieved in Spanish.

A well-known experiment was once carried out with trainee priests. They were individually asked to prepare a short talk about the parable of the Good Samaritan. At the end of their preparation session each trainee was then asked to go over to another building to give his talk. Some were informed that there was plenty of time to get to the other building, others were told to hurry because they were running late and the talk was due to start in a few minutes.

En route to the talk, the experimenters had placed an actor slumped on the ground, head down, eyes closed, moaning and coughing. In the experiment 63 per cent of the group who 'had plenty of time' stopped to help the man, while only 10 per cent of the group who were told they were 'late' stopped to help. Evidently, the convictions of your heart and the actual contents of your thoughts are less important in guiding your actions than the immediate context of your behaviour.

Communicators need to take into account and manage the context in which any message is delivered. Most practitioners when reflecting on earlier successful work tend to suffer from a retrospective myopia, where it was the quality of their genius or good practice that marked out the success of a campaign, rather than the reality of its being greatly assisted by its context.

The influences shaping the context of how ideas are received can be divided into four groups:

- **drivers:** the factors influencing how people accommodate new communications;
- **length of journey:** the distance people have to travel in terms of communications from their existing mental maps to any new perceptions as a result of your communication;
- **dynamics of other memes:** what other memes can do to boost, subsume or make your message bland;

- **socio-economic-political cycles:** the wide-ranging trends which can shape and mould a context.

DRIVERS – GROUP THINK

Want to change your views or alter your perspective on Adolf Hitler, Joseph Stalin or Osama Bin Laden? This challenge might work if your birthday is on 20 April, 21 December or 10 March – the respective birth dates of these well-known figures. Even sharing a birthday with someone can influence how you perceive the person. If you are born on the same day you are more likely to be favourable to him or her. This is caused by 'group power', or what is called 'group think'. Once you are part of a group, you are susceptible to peer pressure, social norms and any number of other kinds of influence brought into play by the group. These are so powerful, they can overwhelm your inherent predispositions. As philosopher Stuart Sutherland observed, with the exception of Groucho Marx, people are essentially clubbable.

The novelist Kurt Vonnegut (1992) coined the name 'Granfalloons', meaning 'proud and meaningless associations of human beings'. It describes a minimum group paradigm, where individuals are formed into groups on the most trivial and inconsequential criteria imaginable. The 18th-century satirist Jonathan Swift also explored this when his character Gulliver in his travels comes across a society divided into 'Big Endians and 'Little Endians', defining themselves by how the groups chose to eat their eggs – either the big or small end first.

In group think there are two basic psychological processes at work. The group first provides the paradigm for making sense of the world. Differences between groups are exaggerated, and similarities within the group emphasized. Second, social groups are a source of self-esteem and pride. To obtain the self-esteem the group has to offer, members defend it, and adopt its symbols, vocabulary, rituals and beliefs. If you accept you are part of the same 'granfalloon' you have strong motivation to defend the group, even if its shared element is something as inconsequential as the same birth date.

The degree to which you are influenced by group think will be affected by how long you perceive the group will be together. If there is a long-term commitment people tend to compromise more because they know they will have another chance over the long term to compensate for any immediate shortcoming. If it is a short-term relationship you will tend to be less flexible, as you might not be around to get a chance to redress the balance.

The skilled public relations communicator will seek to harness potential group think, first by establishing rapport, a commonality of interests with the target (see Chapter 9), and second by harnessing relevant group symbols to further the message.

Task: putting it into practice

What group think are you guilty of? What group think messages can you create for your target audiences? What group think can you identify in any media coverage?

LENGTH OF JOURNEY: THE POWER OF 'HALF-STEPS'

Context also influences successful communications by the distance people have to travel, in terms of moving from their existing mental maps to any new perceptions as a result of your communication.

Winston Churchill would have been regarded as an outright crank had he urged the British people to fight the Germans 'on the beaches ... and never surrender' back in 1936 when Germany reoccupied the Rhineland. Yet his message was perfectly appropriate in Britain's darkest hour in 1940. Would Abraham Lincoln's Gettysburg Address have been in such high regard had it been delivered prior to, rather than during, the American Civil War?

Key influences which shape the context of communications journeys are:

- emergence theory;
- win–win thinking;
- systems feedback;
- contextual influencers: horn and halo effects, inoculation, commonality.

Emergence theory

How far do you want to move people from their existing perceptions and mind states? The longer the journey you need them to take, the more difficult will be your challenge. If there is a simple, low-resistance path to an action (the ideal situation), people are far more likely to adopt it. Imitation is one of the fundamental characteristics of a meme. It is much easier to copy something if the new request is similar to what is there already.

The overall impact and success of a communication is fundamentally determined by its connectivity and close proximity to its potential host environment. The size of gap between your new communication and its context will crucially determine its meme viability.

There is a compelling parallel between biological growth (how life develops), and communications growth (how perceptions change). In his study of Darwinism, Daniel Dennett (1996) highlights the underlying mindlessness guiding biological development. Nature creates brilliant designs: just look at the complexity in a flower or a spider's web, for example. Yet each constituent step in the design process, as well as the transition between steps, is utterly simple – even for an idiot to perform. It requires no wise decisions or delicate judgements or intuitions.

Similarly, a computer program is an algorithm, ultimately composed of simple steps that can be executed with stupendous reliability, by one simple mechanism or another. No matter how impressive the products of an algorithmic development might be, the underlying process always consists of nothing but a set of individually mindless steps succeeding each other without the help of any intelligent supervision. They are automatic by definition, feeding off each other, or on blind chance, and nothing else.

In his book *Emergence*, Steve Johnson (2001) highlighted how Japanese scientists trained a slime mould to find the shortest route in a maze puzzle. Without any evident cognitive resources the slime mould solved the puzzle. Change, whether it involves the example of a slime mould solving a maze puzzle, or complexities of interpersonal relationships, is created by drawing on masses of individual small steps rather than a single, intelligent grand plan.

How does any community emerge? Is it through a well-defined, ordered plan? How does an ant in an ant colony know about the well-defined role it has to play to support the wider good of the colony? Why are towns and cities structured by social class, with their working-class areas, ghettoes and affluent neighbourhoods? These networks are not created by design but are shaped by the emergent properties within them. These emergent properties are defined as elements above and beyond the properties of the parts. You cannot predict the properties of a complete system by taking it to pieces and analysing its parts. Knowledge is gained through analysis; understanding is reached through synthesis of understanding the interdependence of different parts. You would not for example define a cat by dissecting it, and examine and catalogue each of its parts. The living quality and dynamic of the animal is much more than its parts.

Emergent communications are created from bottom-up systems, generated by a multiplicity of many small messages to create a complex adaptive system. Emergent communications move from low-level rules to higher-level sophistication. Yet there is a tendency among communicators to examine a situation from the top-down viewpoint. The key challenge is not necessarily to create an entire message, but to harness the potential for bottom-up communications, moving from the low level to higher levels, by examining what is already there as a message and build from this.

For communicators the fundamental question to be addressed is: what half-steps, from the perspective of the target audience, are needed to move towards changing their behaviours or attitudes? People take a series of small steps in their journey of changing attitudes. Much communications practice fails because it takes too big a step, making too many assumptions about its audience and the context, consequently failing to take people with it. Communicators should ask themselves, what half-steps do I need my target to take? By posing and addressing this question you are more likely to begin a genuine shift in attitudes and behaviours.

Before broadcasting any messages you should analyse the content of your message.

● Is it coherent in its readability, listenability, or visual presentation?
● Does it contain consistent or contradictory messages?
● Does it contain too many themes?
● Does it reflect the values, beliefs and language of the target market?
● Does it address too many publics at once?
● Does it use an appropriate style of argument: one-sided or balanced views?

Making small steps, or half-steps, does not necessarily restrict the potential for diversity in communications. Peter de Vries began his novel *The Vale of Laughter* (1968; quoted in Dennett, 1996) with a variation from the opening of *Moby Dick*: 'Call me, Ishmael.' What a difference a comma can make!

Making one small half-step change can create significant differences. It is rather like the game of Chinese whispers where each generation of the message being passed on introduces a new context, with the potential for the message to be transformed. The old military story of the general receiving the message 'Send three and fourpence, we're going to a dance,' instead of 'Send reinforcements, we are going to advance' is a well-known meme, aptly capturing this dynamic.

Your communication competes for resources to achieve attention, engagement or further replication of the message from the target. Self-replicating messages do not just fall together, with the communications somehow striking lucky in securing coverage. Successful messages capitalize on a balance between their own meme qualities and stimulus to the target, and the order, design and potential for growth in the context. You need just the right sort of order with just the right mix of freedom and constraint, growth and decay, rigidity and fluidity for development to occur.

You need a world where growth is possible yet not too explosive; where higher-order things can move and change, and also retain their identity over time. For any communication to survive it has to succeed in an environment where the message must make sufficient impact on its target; otherwise it will not be adopted. The message goes out alongside numerous other competing messages, crowding out its potential to get registered and be sustainable.

Task: putting it into practice

Reflect back on any recent communications. In what ways did you provide 'half-steps' to create a change of behaviour? In what ways did you fail to introduce 'half-steps' to facilitate change? Review a recent communication. Create new 'half-steps' in your messages.

Win–win thinking

Effective communicators adopt a philosophy of seeking win–win solutions with their target audience. Win–win is a frame of thinking that works to achieve mutual benefits in all transactions, where solutions are beneficial to both sides. The win–win communicator seeks to make all parties feel good about their decision and committed to cooperation with him or her on a quest. Win–win is not achieved at the expense or through exclusion of the success of others.

Most people however tend to think in competitive win–lose terms. There are specific instances where win–lose thinking is required, such as in a competitive event – someone has to win (unless it is a five-day Test cricket match!). Yet most of life is not a competition. How helpful is it to think, 'Who is winning in my marriage?' or 'Who among my colleagues is winning at the expense of my interests?' An abundance mentality recognizes there is plenty in the world for everyone. People with a scarcity mentality have a difficult time sharing recognition, credit, power or profit.

Most of life is interdependent. Human society is underpinned by a philosophy of reciprocal altruism: you do good to others as you expect others to respond likewise. In the long run everyone gains. By thinking, practising and communicating win–win you are minimizing the steps other people need to take to advance your interests. They do not have to make major steps to abandon their own interests in order to advance your cause.

Systems feedback

All communications take place within a 'system'. Your communications are not just in a linear pattern where you say something to your target and their reaction marks a cul de sac in the whole relationship. Every action has a reaction and will affect the parameme in some way.

Systems have two basic types of feedback. The first is *reinforcing feedback*, where changes in the whole system feed back to amplify the original change. Change goes through the system, producing an avalanche effect of more changes in the same direction. The second is *balancing or negative feedback*, where changes in the whole system feed back to oppose the original change, and subsequently dampening its effect.

Fundamental elements to recognize in any systems analysis are:

● You cannot *not* communicate. Whatever you do affects the parameme of a situation in some way.
● Communication is at two levels, containing both content and an interface in your relationships. Communicating is not just what you say, but who you are saying it to, and how this can affect the dynamic of your relationship.
● The chicken and egg paradox – communications does not take place in a vacuum but rather in a parameme, with a legacy of earlier communications and the potential for new memes to be created. Like the 'what comes first' paradox of the chicken and egg, sometimes it can be impossible to identify the specific triggers leading to a mind-state and perceptions, or why people have reacted in certain ways to your communication.
● Communication transactions are between equals or non-equals. You need to take into account the relative status of the partners in the relationship, and how this in turn impacts on the communication.
● Leverage is possible in the system if you know where to intervene to get maximum response from the least effort. The question to ask when examining any system is, 'What is stopping the change?'

A useful tool for assessing a system is force field analysis. This identifies the different forces driving change, along with any obstacles or restraining forces to change. From this analysis any positives can be reinforced and negatives reduced or eliminated.

You need to understand and appreciate the relationships and constraints that can really constrain your potential range of options in a situation. If you learn to read these dynamics it will help you master the processes of creating change in a given situation.

> ### Task: putting it into practice
>
> What factors are holding back the success and effectiveness of your campaign? What would happen if you changed one or more elements? Review a recent campaign and identify the force field elements within it.

Contextual influencers

Halo and horn effects

The 'halo effect' occurs when you form an overall positive impression of someone because of one good characteristic, or his or her association with someone who is trusted and well liked. This positive judgement, or anchor, is carried over into other areas where the person might or might not be competent. By letting your high quality rating in one area let you influence you in other areas, you are in effect being swayed by the person's halo.

If, for example, you describe someone as being like Mother Theresa, the nun who devoted her life to helping the poor, you are seeking to confer Mother Theresa's saint-like qualities on the other person. This effect is often why job interviews are so unreliable for evaluating potential employees. It is also the reason for celebrity endorsement: it is hoped that the glamour and prestige of the personality will positively impact the often completely unrelated product.

Inversely, the 'horn effect' acts as a negative anchor which distorts perception, so positive qualities may be overlooked and overshadowed by unrelated negative attributes. Describing someone as being like a cross between Attila the Hun and Pol Pot will obviously not make him or her appear endearing.

In general, people overestimate personality characteristics and underestimate the importance of context and situation. They are more attuned to personal cues than contextual ones. As a communicator you need to ask, 'What potential benefits can I gain through linking my communication with someone else whose "halo" can benefit my cause?' Alternatively, what 'horn effect' can you create for those opposing you?

Inoculation

You can prepare your targets for your message by pre-positioning them by actively identifying any existing preconceptions, counter-arguments or prejudices. Rather as a medical inoculation works by injecting the subject with a small dose of the contrary material, its communications counterpart uses exactly the same process. Negative views are expressed and factually contextualized: 'You might think this about us but I would like to explain the reason ...'.

Build commonality

If you establish a commonality with your target you can then use this as a platform for any contrary information. Here are some bridge-builders used by the British prime minister Tony Blair, a master of implying that he is agreeing with someone before then going on to disagree with him or her, as these examples from dealing with potential adversaries at a Parliamentary Liaison Committee reveal:

> I don't disagree with the central thrust of what you are saying at all .... I totally sympathize with the problem you are talking about .... I think that's a very reasonable way of putting the point to me .... From your question and the question others have put I suggest there isn't an essential conflict.

> (quoted in the *Independent* by Simon Carr, 7 July 2004)

It is very hard to disagree with someone who is ostensibly agreeing with you.

ROLE OF OTHER MEMES

No meme is an island, replicating in isolation. Other memes can affect your message by giving it a boost, subsume and prevent it from obtaining full recognition, or submerge it in a fog of blandness.

Booster memes

Your message, your meme, could serve other interests. The synergies between the different memes could boost your meme. This tends to happen where you get two memes which happen to be physically tied together, so they always tend to replicate together. A good example is the wedding march music at Christian English weddings. No one insists that this should be the musical entrée at the ceremony. Somehow it has become the considered norm for the event.

Suffocator memes

A rival meme representing a different interest could seek to assert itself and effectively suffocate your message. The story of Richard Cromwell, who ruled the Britain Republic for six months in 1658–9, has been largely neglected in English history teaching. Instead, the historical meme of Britain's royal family and subsequent constitutional monarchy is more prevalent.

Bland memes

Your individual message could be masked by a sea of other similar indistinguishable memes, to effectively render your message bland. The clutter of competing messages in your marketplace creates a bland porridge of me-too messages. Your particular meme is indistinct and subsequently overlooked.

Task: putting it into practice

What competing memes have been evident in any recent communications? Find examples of the different types of memes.

SOCIO-ECONOMIC-POLITICAL CYCLES

The adage by Victor Hugo that 'There is one thing stronger than all the armies in the world, and that is an idea whose time has come' (www.brainyquote.com) rightly emphasizes that no matter how good you might feel your idea or message is, the role of context is all-important.

Communicators operate in environments shaped by social, economic and political factors. These strands do not operate as a continuum but rather in a series of cycles, operating in different timescales. The convergence of these cycles can create a climate of opinion, an environment conducive to certain cultural activity taking place in a particular period. This is perhaps why history records clusters of geniuses, in eras such as the Renaissance and the Enlightenment. 'An idea whose time has come' marks the suitability of the context to be receptive to ideas appropriate for the time.

On a macro scale when you communicate your message there will be similar macro social, economic and political factors at play, not just mirroring global trends also exercising similar dynamics on a pocket-sized scale. Budgets might or might not be available, the political buy-in of

177

particular managers could be crucial, fashions specific to your marketplace could be out of synch with your specific idea. On a much smaller scale, no matter how good your performance as a communicator, the time might just not be right for your particular communications.

COMMUNICATIONS ARE CUMULATIVE

The analogy of the public relations communicator acting like a legal advocate in representing a case and presenting it in the best light possible is flawed. Unlike the legal jury which meets in a one-off episode, the communicator will often have to present to the same audience time and time again. If a communicator sought to gain short-term advantage by misleading, or even lying, he or she would do so at the risk of compromising his or her credibility for subsequent occasions.

Task: putting it into practice

When negotiating, dealing with a conflict situation, or managing a relationship, do you take into account the context not just for you, but also the people you are communicating with? Identify some communications that suffered from being too far ahead of their time, or too late.

OVERVIEW OF THE POWER OF CONTEXT: *MEIN KAMPF*

Let us engage in an exercise to capture the significance of context on the value and impact of any communications, using as an extreme example one of the most powerful memes of the 20th century, Adolf Hitler's *Mein Kampf*, to create two very different outcomes.

Compare the different perspectives on *Mein Kampf* given in Table 10.1 One is from a contemporary liberal humanist view and the other from a hypothetical position of an Aryan national socialist had Hitler been successful, won the Second World War, and subsequently ruled over much of the world.

Mein Kampf is just one book, yet it is able to generate many different reactions, which are determined by the situation of the message and the recipient. Such is the power of context.

Outstanding public relations communicators are creatures partly of their environment: they are able to spot trends, issues which might impact

Table 10.1 *Perspectives on Mein Kampf*

Contextual factors	Liberal humanist perception	If Hitler had won
Groupthink	Hitler was a representative of an evil force outside our group	Hitler was our leader, the Führer and the epitome of 'one of us'
Needs	The book serves a need as a reference source for the historian or political scientist. There is a minority interest from far right-wing supporters. People in liberal democracies supporting extreme politics, beyond the mainstream, may be influenced by needs for their perceived security, self-interests, or self-esteem identified by them to be relevant to their situation.	The book meets the needs of citizens within the Reich for security. By having a copy you highlight your belonging to the same group as those ruling your society. It meets your needs for actualization by providing philosophical insights into the Führer's thoughts.
Belief	Believed to be the work of a despotic madman responsible for perhaps the greatest crimes against humanity	Believed to be the 'Bible' of the man who created the Third Reich
Values	The book is opposite to the values of all people born equal, in a peaceful world, with the German state as an integral member of the European Community of nations	The book gave a philosophical underpinning for accepting the Master Race and Nazi Germany's destiny to rule Europe and the world
Dissonance	Unless you were reading it for a specific academic interest you would probably avoid reading it, with its potential of creating feelings of unease	The book provides a testimony to a position of belonging to greatness and being part of a 'successful' regime. You would not want to dispute the book's content, relevance or literary quality if you wanted to be successful in your society.
Emergence theory	You would need to make a dramatic conceptual leap from your existing perception and mindset to find the book's contents acceptable	Supporting the teachings of the Führer is consistent with your interests in the wider community

Table 10.1 *Perspectives on Mein Kampf (continued)*

Contextual factors	Liberal humanist perception	If Hitler had won
Win–win	If more people were aware of the reality of the teachings in this book, society could prevent history from repeating itself	Reading this book will help you become a better National Socialist
Halo effect	You feel better about yourself by rejecting the teachings of this man	The work is by your Führer, the man responsible for the success of the regime under which you live
Horn effect	Written by one of the most evil rulers in history. Indeed, it is not even well written, being repetitive and hysterical in tone.	Opponents of the regime have a vested interest in undermining the qualities of the Führer
Connectivity	Available (although the dissemination of *Mein Kampf*, like other Nazi symbols, is illegal in Germany) selling an estimated 15,000 copies a year	Every person is been issued with a copy. Its doctrine underpins the education system and it is widely taught in schools

on them, or their organization, ahead of others. They are also able to gain powerful leverage to help their communications from opportunities around them.

PR FUTURES DEBATE

What are the context factors affecting the future of public relations?

Should PR practitioners be recognized as organizational context managers, focusing on managing the environment for organizations?

Should public relations be redefined as 'Public relations is about creating sustainable added value for an organization's reputation by managing its brand, actions, memes and networking'?

PERSONAL CHECKLIST

- What group think is there in your organization?
- What 'halo' and 'horn' effects should you be harnessing?
- What previous personal communication failures can you relate to as a result of overlooking the half-steps your targets need to take?

PRELUDE TO CHAPTER 11

The final chapter seeks to bring together all the different communications elements by contrasting the experience of two young men separated by 2,000 years – the creator of the 'Love Bug' internet virus and Jesus Christ. The concept of 'personal brandcasting' brings together all the elements: where you harness your own personal branding and communication skills to create meme-friendly messages, using their networks to generate a buzz around their message, which in turn can engage mass media to cover the story and further sustain the dynamic of a meme.

Nourishing your ethical passion, doing what you perceive to be the right thing, will provide your communications with immense profound power. Of the most critical DNA sites, 99.4 per cent are identical in humans and chimpanzees – just 0.6 per cent can make a dramatic difference. Your DNA and dreams are unique. You should make the most of them.

11

Bringing it all together

Two young men separated by 2,000 years demonstrate how each of us in public relations has the potential to communicate and change the world in some way. Neither had phenomenal resources, or mass advertising and marketing budgets. They both however used highly effective communications tools which are also available to you. What can be learnt from their experiences?

THE LOVE BUG

Some time on 4 May 2000 unwitting e-mail users discovered what was to be called the 'Love Bug' virus. Within hours it spread to every continent and had wormed its way into tens of thousands of computers. The bug's ability to transmit itself automatically to every infected user's Microsoft Outlook address book made it particularly virulent. The virus was quickly to mutate beyond its original subject line of 'ILOVEYOU: A love letter for you'.

The 'Love Bug' claimed to have reached up to an estimated 45 million computers worldwide, with high-profile victims ranging from the House of Commons to the Pentagon, causing damage reckoned to cost up to US $10 billion to put right. Parallel with the physical spread of the virus was attendant media coverage: it was a prime news story on media around the world.

The alleged mastermind behind the Love Bug was a young Filipino computer student, Onel de Guzman. This son of a fisherman was never prosecuted because Philippine law did not cover the offence he was suspected of committing. Guzman admitted to 'cooking' the virus, and admitted to police that he probably released the virus by accident. Not a great communicator, barely speaking English, he might have been expected to be one of the least likely people to engage and communicate with millions around the world.

Yet his communications had some of the hallmarks essential to outstanding success. Guzman's alleged virus featured a number of icons. It had a memorable name, the 'Love Bug', rather than an obscure, unpronounceable title. The subject of love and romance is something everyone can connect with. Rather than having an obscure name such as virus wm122287, the brand name 'Love Bug' gave it iconic status.

The subject of viruses capitalized on emergence theory. A majority of people know of computer viruses, yet most are not sure what they are, how they work and why they are released into the world. They do however readily know the name 'computer virus', and fear the unknown damage and havoc they can cause. As a result they are readily attuned to the prospect of a threat and will be alert and quick to respond if prompted. Guzman's 'Love Bug' did not consequently require a major conceptual leap to enter people's consciousnesses, only half a step, focusing the underlying fear on to his virus.

Guzman incidentally also emerged as a cult figure among youth in his homeland, a symbol of the new internet age. The young man had become an icon himself of the power of the nerd, the single, unexceptional student able to wreck havoc in the modern communications world.

The 'Love Bug' took advantage of a feature in Windows called Windows Scripting Host, which allows users to automate routine tasks. The virus's author created a Visual Basic script that was directed to send itself to all recipients in a user's Microsoft Outlook address book and then delete image files and hide audio files. Few users actually need the Scripting Host feature but it was turned on by default in Outlook. As one industry expert observed, 'Windows Scripting Host was almost like the 'Virus Scripting Host'.

This inadvertent help given by a Microsoft Outlook facility ultimately gave Guzman's communication great connectivity. In the same way that having a human connector in your network can extend your message with greater velocity to different networks, the Windows Scripting Host acted like a virtual connector and salesperson in computer networks. The original 'Love Bug' message was transmitted and replicated to many more people thanks to these virtual third parties.

Most ideas are not taken on board unless they are adopted and sanctioned by a third party, usually what can be characterized as a gatekeeper to a network of contacts. In the short term the 'Love Bug' virus succeeded in getting a form of virtual endorsement from the computers it hit, which in turn, redirected and sent it on to others.

In the longer term, as a result of virus-detecting software, the virus lost its replicator quality, effectively becoming proscribed and defeated by third parties refusing to accept it or send it on to others. The virus protection equipment worked to prevent its further transmission, acting like a suffocator meme.

Paradoxically, the 'Love Bug' also has a booster meme working to its favour, piggy-backing on the opportunity it presented. The media created its own information virus through its reporting of the story of the 'Love Bug' virus. Was misinformation deliberately created in the media coverage to make it appear more dangerous than it actually was? Just how extensive was the virus in reality, and how much damage did it really create?

Estimates on the scale and cost of the Love Bug vary from 1 million to 45 million machines affected, while the cost of damage ranges from US $1 billion to US $10 billion. As industry pundit Brian Martin cynically observed, anti-virus and security companies and industry media create media interest in stories about viruses, and benefit from the resulting intense awareness of the latest viruses. (This and further views of Brian on viruses and spam mail can be found at www.atrition.org.) The greater the fear of computer viruses, the more people are likely to spend on protection software and systems. Martin notes how an anagram from the words LOVEBUG and an earlier major virus scare MELISSA is BIG VOLUME SALES.

Young Guzman fully harnessed the potential of new media to spread his word worldwide. How did his efforts compare with another young man who created a worldwide message, some two thousand years earlier?

JESUS CHRIST

The story of the Christian church radiates out from the figure of Jesus Christ, the person Christians believe to be the Son of God. Suspend any personal religious beliefs. (Indeed, I could have used many of the leading iconic figures in other religions as examples, since they used similar processes and techniques.) Let us examine the figure of Jesus Christ as a communicator, a public relations practitioner of 2,000 years ago.

In spreading his message Jesus Christ had a profound inner conviction and sense of purpose. His mission was driven by a divine quest to spread what he perceived to be the word of God. It is assumed he possessed extremely good interpersonal skills. Interestingly, the total length of his reported speech in the New Testament is estimated to be just two and a half hours – about the same as a blockbuster movie (figure quoted by 'Father Phil' in the television series *The Sopranos*).

Jesus also had an estimated 40 or 50 other rivals claiming to be the Messiah (a situation wonderfully parodied in the Monty Python film *The Life of Brian*). These rivals could have acted like bland memes to mask his significance and obscure his individual claims to be remembered by history. Yet Jesus's message and meme emerged triumphant from this potential confusion to be remembered to this day.

Jesus lived in a largely illiterate society, which was obviously without modern mass media. He initially used one-to-one encounters and public meetings as his prime communication channels. Jesus's teachings, stored in a coherent and copyable form in the Bible's New Testament, provided the reference resource for the information experts in the network, the mavens, to store and build on his knowledge. Over the centuries new technology has been harnessed, from the use of the written and then printed word, through to television evangelists broadcasting his messages.

In order to explain his new philosophy Jesus used parables, which are reported in the Bible. To feed the hungry five thousand Jesus did not order in bulk supplies, working with the symbolic gesture of feeding the masses with two fishes and five loaves. His story-telling contained profound lessons and moral statements, and also worked to fully engage his audience with his story.

By basing his message around stories he effectively harnessed the power of metaphors. His catalogue of metaphors was able to convince and persuade sceptical unbelievers of the benefits of his new religion. The early Christian church subsequently used the medieval *exemplum,* a brief story to illustrate a particular moral point. These were more effective for conversion of unbelievers than subtle and learned sermons about doctrine.

Jesus's parables also worked as meme-friendly 'sticky messages'. At a time when most of the population was illiterate, communications was based around the oral tradition of story-telling. Stories provide an easily understandable, coherent message, and are capable of being re-told again and again without too much degradation of the original core message.

Sure, there were distortions of the message along the way. Christian scholars accept the mistranslation of the Hebrew word for 'young woman' into the Greek word for 'virgin' as leading to the concept (or misconception) of the story of the virgin birth of Jesus. Although various reprints of the Bible have updated the language used to make it more meme-friendly to contemporary audiences, the core of Jesus's teachings has nonetheless been preserved for nearly 2,000 years.

In his actions Jesus was prepared to die for his convictions. His death marked the ultimate statement of his own faith and also served as a further parable of his sacrifice for humankind's redemption. His behaviours matched his message. He delivered the ultimate congruity in his brand.

Jesus's followers created icons. The image of the cross was an easily memorable and copyable badge which could be replicated extensively. In later centuries the Christian Church built large structures to serve on one level as a meeting point for followers, and on another to symbolize its might, power and status.

Jesus's messages were values-based. They did not just give information about the merits of his perspective on humankind's spiritual dimension, but provided a moral framework, explicitly guiding followers on what is right and not right to do. The values showed how his followers could adopt his specific messages to guide their behaviours in everyday lives, in situations well beyond their original context.

The subject matter of Jesus's teachings dealt with beliefs and spiritual values meeting the highest level of needs in actualization. Enabling believers to achieve actualization could provide a further impetus to getting his message spread. If the path to spiritual self-fulfilment and realizing your potential is through being an evangelist for your cause, then spreading the word about your spiritual wellness makes your message virus-worthy – if you feel something is worth talking about, it will get talked about.

Jesus's teachings met an aesthetic need. They gave coherence to profound questions about the meaning of life. The teachings also met cognitive needs by providing explanations to unfathomable questions like 'How did humankind get here and what is its purpose?'

The rules and procedures of the Christian church created mechanisms for generating self-esteem among adherents. Jesus's followers enjoyed a sense of common purpose, with codes of participation creating a sense of togetherness among believers. Establishing clear rules for those in the group also demarcated those outside the group, from forces to be opposed, rival religions and unbelievers, to the Devil itself – giving the meme coherence and copyability.

Jesus's teachings offer perhaps the most powerful 'what's in it for me?' appeal, with their vision of an after-life and redemption in heaven addressing the great insecurity of what happens to you, your soul and humankind after death. Through its practical programmes of providing alms to the poor or sick, the Christian Church was even able to meet believers' physical needs in times of hunger.

Strong external threats from contemporary pagan rulers acted as a barrier to restrict the connectivity of the Jesus meme: Christians could be killed for their beliefs. Such threats would have inherently curtailed and restricted the spread of the Christian message. Inversely, they would also have entrenched the depth of feeling – the parememe of Christian belief – among its followers. They would have stronger faith to substantiate the dissonance created by the threat of death for their beliefs: if you are going to die for your beliefs you will justify them and make them even stronger to yourself. The subsequent use of rote learning, where members learn sets of beliefs, prayers and key statements, results in the faith becoming embedded in their psyche and resistant to change.

When Jesus literally established a team of disciples they provided the core of his network, acting as connectors and salesmen to spread his word. In later centuries employees of the church, from priests to missionaries, formally circulated Jesus's message. He charged these connectors with a great commission to go forth and spread the word.

Yet just as Jesus has created an intensely powerful meme, it faces competition from rival suffocator memes proffering their own versions of 'the truth', along with a bland meme for non-religious people who switch off from any debate on questions of the after-life and deeper moral issues. Religion now competes alongside materialism, celebritydom and the desire for instant gratification for people's time, attention and engagement.

The Jesus meme has grown phenomenally from just one person. However it now faces a number of challenges. Falling church attendances and a decline in formal religious faith in Christian communities provide evidence of the root paradigm becoming more shallow and its pervasiveness contracting.

Yet, despite this, from just one person who harnessed the power of communications, a worldwide religion was created and has survived over 2,000 years.

THE CONTRASTING PARAMEMES OF THE COMPUTER NERD AND THE SON OF GOD

This study is not meant to imply in any way that Onel de Guzman is comparable to Jesus Christ as a communicator, or in the impact of his communications, a fact clearly evidenced by examining the two men's markedly contrasting par"ememes (see Figures 11.1 and 11.2).

The Love Bug parameme

- Face paradigm: initial extensive worldwide coverage with people directly affected or aware of its threat, and attendant media coverage

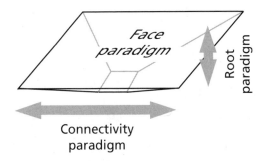

Figure 11.1   *The Love Bug parameme*

publicizing its existence.
- Pervasive paradigm: limited life of the original Love Bug virus. It could live on as an icon in the history of computer viruses.
- Root paradigm: very shallow, with the original virus making transitory impact. Might possibly survive as an iconic reference whenever the

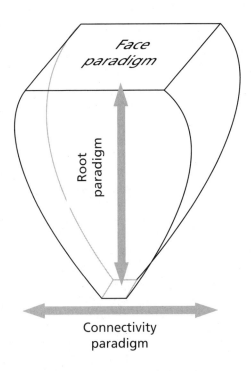

Figure 11.2   *The Jesus Christ parameme*

subject of computer viruses is discussed.

The Jesus Christ parameme

- Face paradigm: extensive worldwide coverage among believers as the son of God, a known religious icon among followers of other faiths and awareness of existence among non-believers.
- Pervasive paradigm: extensive networks and connections although potentially contracting connectivity among believers of his faith in the age of scientific disbelief and materialism.
- Root paradigm: deeply rooted over 2,000 years.

PERSONAL BRANDCASTING: DREAMS, MEMES AND TEAMS

Just think how powerful your communications could be, if you could combine the lessons of the illiterate carpenter and the young Filipino computer student, as well as take advantage of any future opportunities.

You operate in an environment where potentially you can use the latest technology to deliver a message in an instant. Yet it is also an environment of information obesity, with an explosion in channels and messages. The mass communications channels which served the public relations practitioner so well in the late 20th century now appear increasingly fragmented, with questionable credibility. To succeed in this new environment the outstanding communicator will have to resort to different techniques.

Just like Onel de Guzman you can use the power of the internet to communicate in an instant. How can you make your messages and memes sustainable? The successful communicator ironically will return back to basics, to the lessons of the illiterate carpenter of 2,000 years ago: using the power of interpersonal communications, a team of disciples and viral networks, branded communications rich in icons, values and metaphors to make the message meme and w-o-m friendly, to overcome the target's defence barriers and get through with a message perceived as credible.

Although they were separated by two millennia, both men used 'personal brandcasting', creating communications by the way people think, act, create messages and network. (See Figure 11.3.)

For your own personal brandcasting audit you need to ask yourself:

- How strong is your personal or organizational brand based on values and beliefs?
- Are you making full use of every dimension of your personal communications skills?

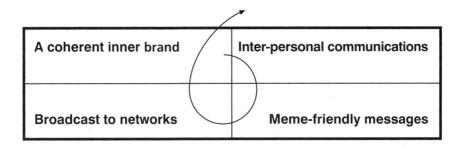

A coherent inner brand	Inter-personal communications
Broadcast to networks	Meme-friendly messages

Figure 11.3 *How personal brandcasting works*

● How coherent and memorable are your messages, based on values and beliefs to make them as sticky and sustainable as possible?
● How effectively are you in engaging the full range of your potential networks?

Jesus Christ fully harnessed the power of beliefs, icons and values, and provided extensive information to substantiate his case. Jesus made the ultimate sacrifice to deliver his message. In his teachings he displayed high-level use of vision, intelligence, emotional and adversity quotients.

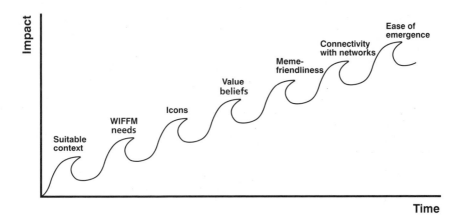

Figure 11.4 *Waves of sustainability for communications*

Jesus's message fully engaged with every dimension of needs levels. (See Figure 11.4.)

How do you make your message sustainable? Great communicators are like surfers, they manage the context of a situation. Great surfers do not necessarily get the first wave. Instead they identify which wave will give them the longest ride. They know how to move from wave to wave in the nimblest manner to maintain their momentum. Surfing is all about tipping points gained from the resourcefulness of a situation.

Outstanding communicators, like great surfers, identify the currents of potential messages and their context. Like the example of Sir Bob Geldof, outstanding communicators believe change is possible, and can radically transform behaviour or beliefs with the right kind of impetus. They start communication epidemics by identifying a selling point which offers a what's-in-it-for-me benefit, creating highly coherent and meme-friendly messages which can be sustained by the values and beliefs of their marketplace.

They concentrate resources on a few key areas, focusing on a selected minority of people to act as their connectors, mavens and salespeople. More people will be reached and engaged to replicate the message if it has an ease of emergence, where it can be easily adopted, requiring their targets to make only a half-step in moving their mental maps of the world.

Leading change activist Carmel McConnell (2003) emphasizes the importance of maximizing your personal resources to overcome the odds:

> For campaigns to succeed, the activist has to be faster and smarter than the institution or individual being challenged. Activists have fewer material resources – certainly in relation to big corporations. So the advantage has to come from inner, rather than outer resources, for example outrageous creativity, the ability to trust and support each other and simple, quiet bravery when it comes to the event. The arrogance of some big firms [hubris] has also been a huge asset to activists.

These qualities hold true not just for the grassroots campaigner but for all public relations practitioners. Even if operating within a large corporation, the individual public relations manager often faces huge resources, or inertia within his or her organization in opposition or resisting change. He or she too has to draw on and make optimum use of his or her personal communications skills similarly to overcome the odds.

A public relations lecturer working in higher education recalls the comments of a college administrator: 'Why is it that whenever there is any trouble at this university your students are involved in it?' This is not to imply that public relations practitioners are troublemakers; the anecdote captures how public relations people are often at the heart of change in any sector and at all levels in society.

What is the fundamental thing practitioners can do to grow, to extend both the impact and significance of their work?

COMMUNICATIONS IS MORE THAN JUST A PRESS RELEASE, PART 2: YOUR PERSONAL MISSION

As a communicator your ability to communicate will be transformed if you are on a mission, where there is congruity between your inner brand, your innermost thoughts, your actions, your messages and the way you connect with your 'teams' and your networks.

Each of us has a power to be in control of our destiny. The father of memes, Professor Richard Dawkins, reflects that although genes and memes have selfish motives, humans still have the power of choice not to be slaves to memes:

> We have the power to defy against the selfish memes of our indoctrination … we are cultured as meme machines, but have the power to turn against our creators. We alone on earth, can rebel against the tyranny of the selfish replicators.
>
> (Dawkins, 1976)

As a professional communicator you should be aware of the responsibilities you carry and the implications of your actions. Perhaps you could take a lesson from advertising legend Bill Bernbach when he appealed, 'All of us who professionally use the media are shapers of society. We can vulgarize that society. We can brutalize it. Or we can help lift it on to a higher level' (www.ciadvertising.org/studies/student/98_fall/theory/weirtz/bernbach.htm).

Another man who faced much hardship in his life yet never stopped short in his bigger quest was the black political activist Dr W E B Du Bois. Speaking to a gathering of friends and family in 1958 he offered some inspiring advice:

> You will find it the fashion …. To judge life's work by the amount of money it brings you. This is a grave mistake. The return from your work must be the satisfaction which that brings you, and the world's need of that work. With this, life is heaven, or as near as heaven as you can get. Without this – with work that you despise, which bores you and which the world does not need – this life is hell …. Income is not greenbacks. It is satisfaction, it is creation; it is beauty. It is the supreme sense of a world of men going forward, lurch and stagger though it may, but slowly, inevitably going forward, and you, you yourself with your hands on the wheels. Make this choice then, my son. Never hesitate, never falter.
>
> (quoted in Bell, 2002)

Nourishing your ethical passion, doing what you perceive to be the right thing, will provide your communications with immense and profound power.

Public relations professionals are uniquely positioned to think intelligently about issues, to use their abilities to create a better future for themselves, their organizations, communities and families – to be good ancestors.

Use the lessons of this book and be an outstanding public relations communicator. Nourishing your ethical passion, doing what you perceive to be the right thing, will provide your communications with immense profound power. Of the most critical DNA sites, 99.4 per cent are identical in humans and chimpanzees – just 0.6 per cent can make a dramatic difference. Your DNA and dreams are unique. You should make the most of them.

The quick read – the jog

Chapter 1

How you think fundamentally shapes what you say, hear and do. Your mind is a unique mental map different from anyone else's, shaped by your beliefs, values and attitudes. Whatever you say or do will be interpreted by other people in some way different from you. Your communication skills are determined by your abilities in intellectual and emotional intelligences, coupled with your vision skills and ability to cope with adversity.

Thinking you are a great communicator is the first stage in being one.

Chapter 2

Your brand of thinking is marked by the qualities and depth of your abilities coupled with your ability to secure the optimum balance between them. You have a communications quotient based on your ability to use your analytical, emotional, vision and adversity quotients. At different times successful communicators call upon different facets and qualities to overcome obstacles to their communications.

Chapter 3

You communicate not just with words or gestures. Neither do you communicate integrity and trust by words. You have a range of languages to convey your messages. Your ears are your best friend.

Chapter 4

Find out how you create messages and how these can live on by acting as memes, which are the currency for exchanging ideas. Perception is reality and you shape your perceptions through paradigms, or 'boxes'. You relate to the world through same-box, small-box or big-box thinking. Discover how by being flexible in your thinking you can secure significant advantage in your communications. Learn that ultimately all ideas are contained in three dimensional boxes, called paramemes.

There are lessons to be learnt from trashy pop songs which you cannot get out of your head.

Chapter 5

The message is the medium. You need to shape your messages to make them meme and brand-friendly. You need to harness the power of icons in your messages to make them distinctive and memorable. You communicate and listen within the structure of a brand, values and beliefs. You need to have clear positionings in your messages. Short is sweet.

Chapter 6

To make things happen your message needs to be trigger-friendly.

You can achieve this by listening, building commonality with your target audience, exploiting benefits, key messages, communicating with flair and flourish, and tailoring your communication as much as possible to the target.

If a picture can paint a thousand words, a metaphor can deliver a million bayonets.

Chapter 7

Word-of-mouth (w-o-m) is the most potent form of communication – pass it on.

W-o-m is perhaps one of the most powerful tools for marketing communications thanks to its credibility, its coming from trusted sources and its ability to replicate like wildfire. W-o-m does not just happen, it can be proactively instigated, stimulated, stretched and boosted to reach many different audiences.

Online communications can also transform your ability to communicate quickly and with many different people to build a critical mass speedily. You need to be aware of the practical limitations of online tools and how they operate in a rapidly changing environment. In this new age of communications everyone can have his or her 15 minutes of fame, or be a 'nonebrity'.

It is reckoned that w-o-m is going to be one of the biggest growth areas in marketing. Communications and public relations professionals should act quickly to seize ownership of this discipline. This is a highly recommended piece of advice.

Chapter 8

Each of us has a variety of networks of contacts. Not everyone is equal in either your networks or other groups you seek to communicate with. By identifying key people you can create a tipping-point effect, a tidal wave of communications. Achieving change with limited resources and the need for any change to be sustainable make partnership working and leveraging action through 'shadow' organizations crucial.

You are probably no more than four contacts away from anyone on this planet.

Chapter 9

Networking is not just about who you know, it is also about who the people you are networking with know. It is often a stepping-stone process rather than a direct hit to reaching your target.

No one is as smart as everyone. Successful networking is not about selling but is based on a philosophy of achieving mutual win–win goals. Networking can be targeted and managed to leverage greater results. Anyone within 12 feet of you provides a networking opportunity. Your business card is your personal brand statement. Networking can be anything from attending business events to running a public relations football team.

Chapter 10

The context in which you present your information determines its value and significance. The successful communicator seeks win–win solutions and gets targets to make 'half-step' moves to change their behaviours. Even sharing a birthday with someone odious can make you change your attitude to them.

Chapter 11

The final chapter seeks to bring all the different communications elements together by contrasting the experience of two young men separated by 2,000 years: the creator of the 'Love Bug' internet virus and Jesus Christ. The concept of 'personal brandcasting' brings together all the elements, where you harness your own personal branding and communication skills to create meme-friendly messages, using their networks to generate a buzz around their message, which in turn can engage mass media to cover the story and further sustain the dynamic of your communication.

Nourishing your ethical passion, doing what you perceive to be the right thing, will provide your communications with immense and profound power. Of the most critical DNA sites, 99.4 per cent are identical in humans and chimpanzees. Just 0.6 per cent can make a dramatic difference. Your DNA and dreams are unique. Make the most of them.

Glossary

adversity quotient   The ability you have to be resilient and overcome adversity.

bigger-box thinking   The term 'outside the box' thinking is erroneously used to describe operating within a bigger paradigm of bigger box thinking.

bland memes   A meme that is barely distinguishable from other competing memes.

booster meme   A meme that assists the promotion of another meme, for example the popularity of the wedding march music in the UK is assisted by a booster meme for promoting a 'traditional wedding'.

bridge building   Rapport technique to get agreement with another by highlighting the points of agreement before raising any points of disagreement.

Captain Scarlet meme   Inspired by the children's television character which was indestructible, a Captain Scarlet meme, like the moon landing hoax, is extremely robust – perhaps indestructible, being able to replicate itself in spite of any profound counter-truths.

communications quotient   The sum of your communication abilities, derived from your adversity, emotional, intelligence and vision quotients.

complacency zone   In contrast to your comfort zone, used to describe relationships and issues in your life to which you have a complacent attitude.

fortean factor   How unusual, odd or different an experience is compared with the target's normal experience.

half-steps   The small steps required for a communications target to move towards a new position.

hibris   An attitude state which is arrogant in its self-belief in delivering a solution but tempered with humility, being prepared to listen to new information from other sources.

icon   The single identifying points you use to label, recognize and relate to something. A key element in defining a brand.

icon absence   Describes a brand with no evident icons.

icon abundance   Describes a brand that has many points of identification: for example New York City inspires a variety of images among different people.

icon singularity   Describes a brand that is known for one single icon.

icon strategy map   Used to identify the different strategies for managing the icons of a brand.

'I'm forever blowing bubbles' syndrome   'I'm forever blowing bubbles' was originally written in 1919 by Jaan Kenbrovin and John William Kellette, a song of its period espousing optimism and overcoming adversity. It soon gained further popularity when it was used to accompany a soap advertisement. Legend has it that supporters of West Ham United Football Club adopted the song in the 1920s because one of the players bore a striking resemblance to the character used in the soap advertisement. Since then, even though performers ranging from George Gershwin to Doris Day have recorded the number in completely different contexts, the song is nowadays evocative in the UK as one of the most powerful and profound football anthems ever. Such is the power of context.

least risk   The key factor in any decision. People do not choose the 'best', they choose what they perceive as 'least risk'.

length of journey   The gap between the present position of the communication target and the desired position.

meme   Originally coined by Richard Dawkins to describe a unit that conveys non-biological information.

nonebrity   Someone who is famous for no outstanding quality.

paradigm   Although the term is conventionally used to describe an overall mind state, it is specifically used in this book to define a boundary of a perception.

parameme   A three-dimensional paradigm used to analyse the communications potential of a meme. It consists of a face, root and connectivity interface.

personal brandcasting   The process of how you create your personal brand, use your interpersonal skills, create memes and use networks potentially to generate tidal waves of communication.

personal sanctum   The closest network each of us has, made up of people whose death would make us feel devastated.

pit stop pessimism   The reality check necessary to evaluate any activity and avoid pessimism becoming permanent or pervasive.

professional sanctum   The closest network of contacts who can influence your professional and business life.

rule number one syndrome   The one personal value that is most important to you and is top of your hierarchy of values.

same-box thinking   Where you operate with the same assumptions as others in a communication.

sanctity paradigm   A platform used in any dialogue, such as 'health and safety', 'national security', 'war on terrorism', where it is difficult for people to argue against the point being made without appearing to compromise their position on these issues.

small-box thinking   Focusing on an element within a bigger paradigm.

spin   Often used as a pejorative term for public relations communications. Consists of minimizing or maximizing the significance of a piece of information, or masking it with something else.

suffocator meme   A meme which competes with another meme to suppress or destroy the competing meme's circulation.

3D thinking   Going beyond the traditional communications model of sender and recipient. It recognizes the dynamic meme-quality of a message to develop its own dynamic and live on beyond the original sender and recipient.

vacillator   An attitude in a state of flux, not in a victim, hubris or hibris state.

vision quotient   The ability to create a horizon, a general sense of direction to your activities, including setting more specific future goals.

voal   A lack of clarity in thinking between a 'vision' and a 'goal'.

w-o-c   Shorthand for online word-of-click communications.

w-o-m   Shorthand for word-of-mouth communications.

Bibliography and further reading

So you want to find out more?

Finding out about your inner brand

Much of the insight for this came from neuro-linguistic programming (NLP) teaching. A good introduction to the subject is *Training with NLP* (O'Connor and Seymour, 1994). Martin Seligman's *Learned Optimism* (1998) offers a great insight into pervasive and permanent pessimism. Despite its naff title and dated style, Dale Carnegie's *How to Win Friends and Influence People* (1953) is still worth visiting for any student who wants to understand how to motivate people. Malcolm Gladwell's *Blink* (2005) makes a persuasive plea for all of us to trust our intuition.

Building your own personal brand

There has been a flurry of books on the subject of personal brands. Perhaps the best example of someone creating a brand out of creating your own brand is Peter Montoya (Montoya and Vandehey, 2002), although some of his later titles I feel over-dilute his core material.

Other titles range from Tom Peter's staccato-like views in *The Brand You 50* (1999) to Thomas Gad and Annette Rosencreutz, *Managing Brand Me* (2002) and Eleri Sampson's *Build Your Personal Brand* (2002).

Interpersonal communications

A comprehensive guide is offered by Owen Hargie and David Dickson's *Skilled Interpersonal Communications* (2004). Also useful is Peter Hartley's *Interpersonal Communications* (1999). Larry Reynolds' *The Trust Effect* (1998) is good for examining how we communicate trust. Graham Lancaster's *The 20% Factor* (1993) provides a general guide to self-improvement, and John Foster's *Effective Writing Skills* (2001) lives up to its title.

Communications theory

The standard texts are curiously devoid of any coverage of memes. The usual suspects for this subject are *McQuail's Mass Communication Theory* by Denis McQuail (2002) and *Using Communication Theory* by Sven Windhal and Benno Signitzer with Jean T Olson (2000). Richard M. Perloff's *The Dynamics of Persuasion* (1993) covers much of the conceptual ground on the structure of communications.

Memes and paradigms

The best overview of memes is *The Meme Machine* by Susan Blackmore (1999). Richard Dawkins's *The Selfish Gene* (1976) first launched the word 'meme' into the world, and his ideas are further developed in *The Extended Phenotype* (1999). Another extremely thought-provoking writer is Daniel C Dennett, whose *Darwin's Dangerous Idea* (1996) is also a must. Robert Aunger also elaborates on the implications of memes in *The Electric Meme* (2002).

Similarly to Dawkins's role in memes, Thomas S Kuhn's *The Structure of Scientific Revolutions* (1996) sets the agenda for the concept of paradigms. Also covering paradigmatic thinking is Jordan B Peterson's *Maps of Meaning* (1999). My own *Creativity in Public Relations* (Green, 2001) provides tools for deconstructing paradigms.

Linking together the worlds of chaos theory and marketing is Winslow Farrell's *How Hits Happen* (1998). Stuart Sutherland's *Irrationality* (1992) is a great read and will ensure you are never tolerant of the 'thin end of the wedge' argument.

Shaping your message

Terence Deacon's *The Symbolic Species* (1997) provides many of the theoretical references to the impact of the development of language on communications. Al Ries and Jack Trout, *Positioning* (2001) is a marketing classic.

Much is owed to Robert B Cialdini's *Influence* (2001) for his insight into persuasion. Luke Sullivan's *Hey, Whipple Squeeze This!* (2003) and Paul Arden's *It's Not How Good You Are, It's How Good You Want to Be* (2003) provide a good insight into the work of creative communicators. Doug Hall's *Jump Start Your Business Brain* (2002) will transform your analysis of benefit propositions.

John Grant's *After Image* (2002) offers stimulating insights on contemporary brand development. Anthony Pratkanis and Elliot Aronson's *Age of Propaganda* (2001) is a good combination of historical case studies and the psychological processes of communication.

Word-of-mouth/viral

I have heard that Seth Godin is one of the leading gurus in this area. Tell your friends about his *Unleashing the Idea Virus* (2002). Other titles in this area include Aaron Lynch's *Thought Contagion* (1996), the entertaining and insightful George Silverman's *The Secrets of Word-Of-Mouth Marketing* (2001) – which possibly contains the worst marketing joke ever about 'the Emperor has no close!' – along with Emanuel Rosen's *The Anatomy of Buzz* (2001). Ryan Mathews and Watts Wacker, *The Deviant's Advantage* (2003) and *Buzz* by Marian Salzman, Ira Matathia and Ann O'Reilly (2003) contain many examples of viral campaigns in action. Michael E Cafferky, *Let Your Customers Do the Talking* (1996) has many practical tips.

E and online communications

It is still early days for in-depth writing on the subject of e-marketing. *Online Public Relations* by David Phillips (2003) is a good introduction. Useful tips can be found in Russell Goldsmith's *Viral Marketing* (2002) and Richard Perry and Andrew Whitaker's *Viral Marketing in a Week* (2002).

Networks

Malcolm Gladwell's *The Tipping Point* (2002) is a must (says he in connector/salesman and maven mode). Ryan and Gross's classic 'The diffusion of hybrid seed corn in two Iowa communities' is described in Rogers, *Diffusion of Innovations* (1995). Laura Berman Fortgang covers immediate personal networks in *Take Yourself to the Top* (1999). A humorous take on building your own network is Danny Wallace's *Join Me: The true story of a man who started a cult by accident* (2003).

Networking

John Timperley's *Network Your Way to Success* (2002) is one of the best summaries. The subject is dominated by American-based texts such as Ivan R Misner and Don Morgan's *Masters of Networking* (2000) and Sandy Vilas and Donna Fisher's *The Power of Networking* (1999). Personal selling skills are also covered by John Timperley in *Connective Selling (2004)* and Ford Harding's *Cross-Selling Success* (2002)

Context

Steve Johnson's *Emergence* (2001) provides an introduction to bottom-up systems. Joseph O'Connor and Ian McDermott, *The Art of Systems Thinking* (1997) provides a good introduction to holistic thinking. Win–win thinking is extolled through Stephen R Covey's *The Seven Habits of Highly Effective People* (1994). There is an extensive choice of works from Anthony Robbins (eg 2001) on personal goal setting. Mihaly Csikszentmihalyi's *Creativity* (1997) contains original research into the lives and attitudes of creative people.

Change activists

Among the new crop of books covering this subject are Carmel McConnell's *Change Activist* (2003) and *Innervation* (2001).

Future of communications

Stimulating reads on future trends and issues are provided by Gary Hamel and C K Prahalad, *Competing for the Future* (1994), Marcus Buckingham and Curt Coffman's *First Break all the Rules* (2000), Charles Leadbeater's *Living on Thin Air* (2000) and Richard Florida, *The Rise of the Creative Class* (2002).

Ethics

Profound insight is offered by two men who in different ways have reconciled overcoming adversity with a higher mission in life: Derrick Bell in *Ethical Ambition* (2002) and Viktor E Frankl in *Man's Search for Ultimate*

Meaning (2002). A good summary of managing the ethical challenges facing practitioners is *Ethics in Public Relations* by Patricia J Parsons (2004).

Wonderful human being and communicator

Please read *The Book of Gossage* (1995), a tribute to the late Howard Gossage, 'the Socrates of San Francisco', who led an inspirational life as a creative communicator. May we achieve a fraction of his greatness in our work.

REFERENCES

Arden, Paul (2003) *It's Not How Good You Are, It's How Good You Want to Be*, Phaidon, London

Aunger, Robert (2002) *The Electric Meme*, Simon & Schuster, London

BBC (2003) *Football Confidential*, various authors, BBC Books, London

Bell, Derrick (2002) *Ethical Ambition*, Bloomsbury, London

Blackmore, Susan (1999) *The Meme Machine*, Oxford University Press, Oxford

Buckingham, Marcus and Coffman, Curt (2000) *First Break All the Rules*, Simon & Schuster, New York

Cafferky, Michael E (1996) *Let Your Customers Do the Talking*, Upstart Publishing, Chicago, IL

Carnegie, Dale (1953) *How to Win Friends and Influence People*, Cedar Books, Tadworth, Surrey

Cialdini, Robert B (2001) *Influence: Science and practice*, Allyn & Bacon, Needham Heights, MA

Covey, Stephen R (1994) *The Seven Habits of Highly Effective People*, Simon & Schuster, London

Csikszentmihalyi, Mihaly (1997) *Creativity: Flow and the psychology of discovery and invention*, HarperCollins, New York

Dawkins, Richard (1976) *The Selfish Gene*, Oxford University Press, Oxford

Dawkins, Richard (1999) *The Extended Phenotype*, Oxford University Press, Oxford

Deacon, Terence (1997) *The Symbolic Species*, Penguin, London

Dennett, Daniel C (1996) *Darwin's Dangerous Idea*, Penguin, London

De Vries, Peter (1968) *The Vale of Laughter*, Gollancz, London

Diamond, Jared (2005) *Collapse: How societies choose to fail or survive*, Penguin, London

Dyke, Greg (2004) *Inside Story*, HarperCollins, London

Farrell, Winslow (1998) *How Hits Happen*, Orion Business Books, London

Florida, Richard (2002) *The Rise of the Creative Class*, Basic Books, New York

Fortgang, Laura Berman (1999) *Take Yourself to the Top*, Thorsons, London

Foster, John (2001) *Effective Writing Skills*, Kogan Page, London

Frankl, Viktor E (2002) *Man's Search for Ultimate Meaning*, Perseus, New York

Gad, Thomas and Rosencreutz, Annette (2002) *Managing Brand Me*, Pearson Education, Harlow

Gardner, Howard (2000) *Intelligence Reframed: Multiple intelligences for the 21st century*, Basic Books, New York

Gladwell, Malcolm (2002) *The Tipping Point*, Bay Back Books, London

Gladwell, Malcolm (2005) *Blink*, Allen Lane, London

Godin, Seth (2002) *Unleashing the Idea Virus*, Simon & Schuster, London

Godin, Seth (2003) *Purple Cow*, Penguin, London

Goldsmith, Russell (2002) *Viral Marketing*, Pearson Education, Harlow

Goleman, Daniel (1996) *Emotional Intelligence*, Bloomsbury, London

Gossage, Howard (1995) *The Book of Gossage*, Copy Workshop, Chicago, IL

Grant, John (2002) *After Image*, Harper Collins, London

Green, Alan (2001) *Creativity in Public Relations*, Kogan Page, London

Hall, D (2002) *Jump Start Your Business Brain*, David & Charles, Newton Abbot

Hamel, Gary and Prahalad, C K (1994) *Competing for the Future*, Harvard Business School, Boston, MA

Harding, Ford (2002) *Cross-Selling Success*, Adams Media, Avon, MA

Hargie, Owen and Dickson, David (2004) *Skilled Interpersonal Communications*, Routledge, Hove

Hartley, Peter (1999) *Interpersonal Communications*, Routledge, London

Howard, Jane (1984) *Margaret Mead: A life*, Simon & Schuster, London

Johnson, Steve (2001) *Emergence*, Penguin, London

Kuhn, Thomas S (1996) *The Structure of Scientific Revolutions*, University of Chicago Press, Chicago, IL

Lancaster, G (1993) *The 20% Factor*, Kogan Page, London

Leadbeater, Charles (2000) *Living on Thin Air*, Penguin, London

Lynch, Aaron (1996) *Thought Contagion*, Basic Books, New York

Lynn, M (nd) *Mega Tips: Scientifically tested techniques to increase your tips* [Online] www.people.cornell.edu/pages/wm13/pdf/megatips.pdf

Maslow, A (1954) *Motivation and Personality*, Harper & Row, New York

Mathews, Ryan and Wacker, Watts (2003) *The Deviant's Advantage*, Random House, London

McConnell, Carmel (2001) *Innervation: Innovate where it counts. Inside*, Pearson Education, Harlow

McConnell, Carmel (2003) *Change Activist: Make big things happen fast*, Pearson Education, Harlow

McLuhan, M and Fiore, Q (2000) *The Medium is the Message*, Gingko Press, Corte Madera, CA

McQuail, Denis (2002) *McQuail's Mass Communication Theory*, Sage, London

Mehrabian, A (1972) *Nonverbal Communications*, Aldine-Atherton, Chicago, IL

Milgram, S (1967) The small world problem, *Psychology Today*, **22**, pp 61–67 details

Miller, G A (1956) The magical number seven, plus or minus two; some limits on our capacity for processing information, *Psychological Review*, **63**, pp 81–97

Misner, Ivan R and Morgan, Don (2000) *Masters of Networking*, Bard Press, Marietta, GA

Montoya, Peter and Vandehey, Tim (2002) *The Brand Called You: The ultimate brand-building and business development handbook to transform anyone into an indispensable personal brand*, Personal Brand, Tustin, CA

Nisbett, R L and Ross, L (1980) *Human Inference*, Prentice-Hall, NJ

Oborne, Peter and Walters, Simon (2004) *Alistair Campbell*, Aurum Press, London

O'Connor, Joseph and McDermott, Ian (1997) *The Art of Systems Thinking*, Thorsons, London

O'Connor, Joseph and Seymour, John (1994) *Training with NLP*, Thorsons, London

Ogilvy, David (2004) *Confessions of an Advertising Man*, Southbank Publishing, London

Parsons, Patricia J (2004) *Ethics in Public Relations*, Kogan Page, London

Perloff, Richard M (1993) *The Dynamics of Persuasion*, Lawrence Erlbaum, Hillsdale, NJ

Perry, Richard and Whitaker, Andrew (2002) *Viral Marketing in a Week*, Hodder & Stoughton, London

Peters, Tom (1999) *The Brand You 50: Reinventing work*, Knopf, New York

Peterson, Jordan B (1999) *Maps of Meaning*, Routledge, London

Phillips, David (2003) *Online Public Relations*, Kogan Page, London

Pitcher, George (2003) *The Death of Spin*, Wiley, Sussex

Pratkanis, Anthony and Aronson, Elliot (2001) *Age of Propaganda*, Freeman, New York

Reynolds, Larry (1998) *The Trust Effect*, Nicholas Brealey, London

Ries, A and Trout, J (2001) *Positioning*, McGraw-Hill, New York

Robbins, Anthony (2001) *Unlimited Power*, Pocket Books, New York

Rogers, E (1995) *Diffusion of Innovations*, Free Press, New York

Rosen, Emanuel (2001) *The Anatomy of Buzz*, Harper Collins, London

Ryan, B and Gross, N (1943) The diffusion of hybrid seed corn in two Iowa communities, *Rural Sociology*, **8**, pp 15–24

Saatchi, Charles (2005) If this is conservatism, I am a conservative – how I lost the election, pamphlet for Centre for Policy Studies, June

Saltzman, Marian, Matathia, Ira and O'Reilly, Ann (2003) *Buzz*, Wiley, NJ

Sampson, Eleri (2002) *Build Your Personal Brand*, Kogan Page, London

Seligman, Martin (1998) *Learned Optimism*, Simon & Schuster, New York

Silverman, George (2001) *The Secrets of Word-Of-Mouth Marketing*, Amacom, New York

Steel, Mark (2002) *Reasons to be Cheerful*, Scribner, London

Sullivan, Luke (2003) *Hey, Whipple Squeeze This!*, Wiley, Hoboken, NJ

Sutherland, Stuart (1992) *Irrationality*, Penguin, London

Timperley, John (2002) *Network Your Way To Success*, Piatkus, London

Timperley, John (2004) *Connective Selling*, Capstone, London

Vilas, Sandy and Fisher, Donna (1999) *The Power of Networking*, Harper-Collins, London

Vonnegut, Kurt (1992) *Wampeters, Foma and Granfalloons*, Bantam Double-day Dell, London

Wallace, Danny (2003) *Join Me: The true story of a man who started a cult by accident*, Random House, London

Wheen, Francis (2004) *How Mumbo Jumbo Conquered the World*, Harper Collins, London

Windhal, Sven and Signitzer, Benno with Olson, Jean T (2000) *Using Communication Theory*, Sage, London

Networking contacts of the author

Michael Bland. Michael and I frequently bump into each other lecturing at various conferences.

Mark Borkowski, whom I first met up with at an industry awards event. We have been soul mates ever since.

Gerry Carson, met Andy at a conference where Andy was the guest speaker.

Simon Collister, who attended an event at my Media Centre in Wakefield. We immediately developed new ideas to work together, culminating in an exhibition challenging images of epilepsy.

Regan Cooper, former head of community affairs at Yorkshire Electricity plc. He was also an ace goalkeeper in a public relations football team I set up, where we first met.

John Drummond, whom I met at a conference where we were both speaking.

Marc Evans, whom I first met when he came to talk to my regional group of the CIPR.

Lorraine Forrest-Turner, whom I met as a fellow member of the group of trainers used by the CIPR.

Pat Gaudin, whom I have met at many CIPR and local government conferences.

Andy Gilbert, was initially connected with Andy through Steve McDermott.

Ian Green, no relation, and my business partner in GREEN communications. (The story goes that I did not want to change my letterhead so I offered Ian the job.)

Andrea Hall, a valued client for several years.

Deborah Heindley, a former client of my PR business.

Sue Johansson, a former colleague of a client of mine. I once gallantly paid for her train fare when Sue had her purse stolen at Kings Cross Station, London and I happened to be in the ticket queue.

Helen Kettleborough, who was a client of mine before she changed jobs, and has kept in touch since.

Will Kintish, a consummate networker whom I met through network contacts.

Jackie Le Fevre, whom I originally met when she was a delegate on one of my creativity training courses.

Steve McDermott, is a former colleague of Andy's who has provided much inspiration and valuable networking contacts since.

Adrian Mahoney, whom I met up with through his work on the Scottish Group of the IPR, to which I am a frequent visitor for lectures and training events.

Andrew Mann, a colleague of one of the players in my PR football team. He then became a client, and still keeps in touch several job moves later.

Theresa Merrick, who first heard me talk at a conference then became a client for my creativity business.

Mike Morgan, whom I met at a conference where we were both speaking.

David Morgan Rees, once a fellow committee member of the CIPR's Yorkshire and Lincolnshire Group.

Kate Nicholas, publisher and formerly editor-in-chief of the UK trade magazine *PR Week*, whom I have met at numerous industry events.

John O'Grady, a colleague of another of the players in my PR football team. He then became a client, and still keeps in touch several job moves later.

William Ostrom, whom I first met when I was a judge in an industry awards. I interviewed William as part of the evaluation procedure.

Gareth Owen, whom a mutual friend referred me to, leading to a number of joint projects.

Alan Preece, currently director of marketing and communications at the University of East Anglia and a former head of public relations at Asda plc. He too is an alumnus of the public relations football team.

Michael Regester, whom I first met at a conference in Zimbabwe at which we were both speaking. We meet up every year at the CIPR Fellows' lunch.

Paul Richards. I came across a reference to Paul in a trade magazine, tracked him down on the internet and got in touch with him.

Barry Sheerman MP. I was a student of Barry's when he lectured at Swansea University and we have stayed in touch ever since.

Douglas Smith. I cannot remember the first time I met Douglas. His mind has been similarly blank after subsequent meetings, particularly the Leo lunches he organizes as a tribute to the outstanding PR talent born under this sign.

Steve Sowerby, gave a talk which included the example used in this book for a networking event Andy attended.

David Taylor, who once spotted a partnership opportunity to work with me. He has since become a partner in my creativity consultancy, creativity@work.

Kevin Taylor, a predecessor of mine at South Yorkshire County Council. Colleagues described my London accent as 'You sound just like Kevin Taylor.' We actually made contact through a mutual colleague seven years later.

John Timperley. When he first came to Leeds to open up a branch office of a public relations consultancy in the city, being a new boy in town, he contacted the local CIPR group enquiring if anyone on the committee would spare him some time to meet informally and provide the low-down on his new patch. I was ostensibly a 'competitor' but I arranged to meet up with him and we have been friends ever since. John has gone on to become a marketing guru with several excellent books to his name.

Robin Wight, was recommended to me as 'someone sharing a passion for memes' by Mike Morgan.

Heather Yaxley, who runs the motor industry Public Affairs group and booked me for a training workshop on 'Funky thinking'. We have since shared several conference platforms.

David Yelland, whom I made a point of introducing myself to at a conference where we were both speaking.

Index